Also by BRETT RUTHERFORD

POETRY
Songs of the I and Thou (1968)
City Limits (1970)
The Pumpkined Heart: Pennsylvania Poems (1973, 2019)
Whippoorwill Road: The Supernatural Poems (1985 to 2012, five editions)
Thunderpuss: In Memoriam (1987)
Prometheus on Fifth Avenue (1987, 2018)
At Lovecraft's Grave (1988)
In Chill November (1990)
Poems from Providence (1991, 2011)
Twilight of the Dictators (with Pieter Vanderbeck) (1992, 2009)
Knecht Ruprecht, or the Bad Boy's Christmas (1992)
The Gods As They Are, On Their Planets (2005, 2012, 2018)
Things Seen in Graveyards (2007, 2017)
Doctor Jones and Other Terrors (2008)
Anniversarius: The Book of Autumn (1984 to 2011, four editions)
An Expectation of Presences (2012)
Trilobite Love Song (2014)
Crackers at Midnight (2018)

PLAYS
Night Gaunts: An Entertainment Based on the Life and Work of H.P. Lovecraft (1993, 2005)

NOVELS
Piper (with John Robertson) (1985, 2018)
The Lost Children (1988, 2018)

AS EDITOR/PUBLISHER
May Eve: A Festival of Supernatural Poems (1975)
Last Flowers: The Romance Poems of Edgar Allan Poe and Sarah Helen Whitman (1987-2011, four editions)
M.G. Lewis's *Tales of Wonder*. Annotated edition. (2 vols, 2010, 2012)
A.T. Fitzroy. *Despised and Rejected*. Annotated edition. (2010)
Death and the Downs: The Poetry of Charles Hamilton Sorley. Annotated edition (2010, 2017)
Tales of Terror: The Supernatural Poem Since 1800. (2 vols, 2015-2016)
Break Every Bond: Sarah Helen Whitman in Providence (2019)
The Writings of Emilie Glen (4 vols, 2009-2017)

THE DOLL WITHOUT A FACE

NEW POEMS & REVISIONS 2018-2019

BRETT RUTHERFORD

The Poet's Press

PITTSBURGH, PA

*Copyright © 2019 by Brett Rutherford
All Rights Reserved*

*The author places this work in the Public Domain
on January 1, 2031.*

Rev 1.2

This is the 241st publication of
THE POET'S PRESS
2209 Murray Avenue #3/ Pittsburgh, PA 15217
www.poetspress.org

TABLE OF CONTENTS

The Girl on the Library Steps   9
The Day Is Normal in My City   11
El Día Es Normal en La Cuidad   12
With Poe on Morton Street Pier (Anniversarius V)   14
Let Them Play! (Anniversarius XLIII)   16
Death and the Maiden, *after Claudius*   20
The Place of Attics   21
At the Edge of the Lake (Anniversarius XLIV)   25
Getting Your Eye   27
The Witches and the High-Court Judge, *after Ben Jonson*   28
The Cemetery at Eylau, 1807   31
The Tea Party   36
First H.P. Lovecraft Waterfire, Providence   39
I Dreamt I Was Dante   41
At the Grave of Homer   43
The Doll Without A Face   44
The Sorcerer's Complaint   50
The Warning   52
A Toast to Wendy   53
The Poet Who Starved, *after Uhland*   60
By A Roman Road Forgotten, *after Yevtushenko*   62
An Old Flame   65
The Partisan's Woman   66
Love Song in Finland, *after Goethe*   68
Finnische Lied (1810)   *Johann Wolfgang von Goethe*   69
Through Mirrors   70
Only An Apple, *after Plato*   71
Why Poetry?   72
The Warning of Solon the Athenian, *from the Greek*   75
The Rage of Athena At Troy, *from Euripides*   78
Writer's Block   81
Out-Home Summers   85
Who Cares to Listen to Songs? *from Akhmatova*   91

A Haight-Ashbury Autumn   92
The Plasma Physicist Explains   93
On Rhyming Poetry   95
Wotan Meets Siegfried   97
At the Top of the World   99
The Autumn Fungus   101
Congress, In Recess   103
The Virgin Mary, After One View of the Kama Sutra   104
The Return of Richard Nixon   107
Moving Day   109
Life Without Siegfried   111
To Cyrnus, *from the Greek of Theognis*   115
What Men Are Like   116
At First Sight   117
When the Vampire Is King   119

ABOUT THE POEMS   121

ABOUT THE POET   129

ABOUT THIS BOOK   130

THE DOLL WITHOUT A FACE

The Girl on the Library Steps

Out I came from the double-door,
arms full of science-fiction adventures,
squinting to see the steep steps downward,
and there I saw her, rail-thin and shabby
as I was, goggle-eyed spectacles
owling up to the library entrance.
She did not move. I squeezed past
through the street door to the leaf-blown sidewalk.

> *Only one book you need ever read,*
> her Pa told her. He slapped the Bible
> against his knee, the leather binding
> just like the strap he used to whip her.

Exultant I flew through the double door.
I swear it opened without my touching.
They had let me into the open stacks —
I had the principal's note averring
that I, a lowly third-grader,
could read at the 12th-grade level.
Hugged to my chest were Goethe's *Faust*,
the dreamt-of *Dracula* at last,
and a tattered copy of *Frankenstein*.
And there she was, on the third step now.
One of her shoes was not like the other.

> *Your cousin Gracie, she was a reader,*
> *least till she got ideas and run away.*
> *They found her dead, and pregnant.*
> *Nobody here'd go to her funeral.*

One book, just one book this time,
a thousand pages of delicious revenge.
Down stairs I almost levitated,
the book already open —
The Count of Monte Cristo. Had I opened
the double-glass door? I think I went
straight through like a house-ghost. Step five

was where I nearly collided with her,
the girl in the home-sewn blue calico dress,
her bare arms a patchwork of bruises.

> *Your Pa found those comic books*
> *your girl-friends loaned you. He says*
> *they're the Devil's work. He burned them.*

One winter Saturday, Shakespeare in hand,
I bellow, "Friends, Romans, countrymen!"
from open page to the empty stairwell.
Oh, she was there in December dark,
the same dress, same mis-matched shoes.
Now that I wore glasses, too,
our vision connected in focus.
We were on the seventh step.
She stared at the book in my hand
and trembled. I told her the story
of *Julius Caesar,* then hurried on.

> *You want a card, a library card?*
> *Your teacher says you need it?*
> *We'll not have you there, unsupervised.*
> *There might be Jews and Catholics.*
> *Library card! Next thing you know*
> *you got some card says you're a Communist!*

"Intelligences vast, cool, and unsympathetic" —
I rolled the words on my tongue as I left
the library with *The War of the Worlds.*
Martians, oh, let the Martians come!
And here, on the uppermost step,
I was nose to nose with the girl again.
I could smell stern soap, and vinegar.
Her blond hair was braided to strangulation.
I held the door open for her.
She did not move. She trembled
"I can't," she said. "I just can't."
I never saw her again.

The Day Is Normal in My City

The day is normal in my city.
In the garden, Manuel is working,
and in the nursery, Celia warms
milk and prepares bedtime stories.
The children have not disappeared.

The lady chooses among three gowns.
The gentleman selects a red necktie.
They are going to the concert hall,
and there, in a walled garden,
behind brick-work and iron gates,
the man will clench his hand
(his cigar is not permitted),
while the lady sips her Sauvignon Blanc.

They will hear the Emperor Concerto.
They will listen to a grand *Te Deum*
with three hundred performers.
Up in the high balcony's cheap seats
the mothers of the children's chorus will smile.
Their children have not disappeared.

After the applause dies off,
the well-dressed crowd flows down
the grand staircase.
The day is normal in my city,
but the unanswered question hangs
like an ominous storm cloud:
You, sir, you, madame! Did you vote for *him?*
Your children have not disappeared.

El Día Es Normal En La Ciudad

El día es normal en la ciudad.
Manuel, en el jardín, trabaja,
y Celia, en el cuarto de los niños,
calienta la leche, y ensaya
los cuentos de hadas.
Los niños no han desaparecido.

La ama de casa elige entre tres vestidos.
El esposo escoge una corbata roja.
Van al teatro para escuchar un concierto.
Y allí, en un jardín amurallado
detrás de ladrillos y puertas de hierro,
el señor apretará la mano
(su cigarro no está permitido),
mientras la señora sorbe un Sauvignon Blanc.

Oirán el Concierto "El Emperador."
Escucharán un Te Deum grande
con trescientos ejecutantes.
Las madres del coro de niños
sonreirán desde el balcón superior.
Sus niños no han desaparecido.

Después que el aplauso se apague,
bien vestidos, la audiencia
fluye por la gran escalera.
El día es normal en la ciudad,
pero la pregunta sin respuesta
se cuelga como nube de tormenta.
Tú, señor, tú, señora — ¿Votaron por *él?*
Tus niños no han desaparecido.

ANNIVERSARIUS V:
WITH POE ON MORTON STREET PIER

Sunset at the Manhattan piers: gray-black,
the iron-cloaked sky splays vortices of red
into the Hudson's unreflecting flow.
Blown west and out by a colorless breeze,
the candle of life falls guttering down
into a carmine fringe above oil tanks,
a warehoused cloud of umber afterglow,
hugging the scabrous shore of New Jersey,
a greedy smoker enveloped in soot.

To think that Poe and his consumptive Muse
stood here in April, Eighteen Forty-Four,
his hopes not dashed by a rainy Sunday —
an editor thrice, undone, now derelict,
author of some six and sixty stories,
his fortune four dollars and fifty cents.
Did he envision his ruin, and ours?
Did his Eureka-seeking consciousness
see rotted piers, blackened with creosote?
Did rain and wind wash clean the Hudson's face,
or was it already an eel-clogged flux
when he came down the shuddering gangplank?

Who greeted him? This feral, arched-back cat,
fish-bone and rat-tail lord of the landing?
Did he foresee the leather'd lonely wraiths
who'd come to the abandoned wharf one day
in a clank-chain unconscious parody
of drugged and dungeon-doomed Fortunato
and his captor and master Montresor?

He gazed through rain and mist at steeple tops,
warehouse and shop and rooming house — to him
our blackened brickwork was El Dorado.
He needed only his ink to conquer
the world of Broadway with his raven quills —
Gotham would pay him, and handsomely, too!

Did the lapping waters deceive him thus —
did no blast of thunder peal to warn him
that this was a place of rot and rancor?
The city shrugs at the absolute tide.
I am here with all my poems. I, too,
have only four dollars and fifty cents
until tomorrow's tedium pays me
brass coins for passionless hours of typing.
I am entranced as the toxic river
creeps up the concrete quay, inviting me,
a brackish editor hungry for verse,
an opiate and an end to breathing.

Beneath the silted piles, the striped bass spawn,
welfare fish in their unlit tenements.
A burst of neon comes on behind me,
blinks on the gray hull of an anchored ship —
green to red to blue light, flashback of fire
from window glaze, blinking a palindrome
into this teeming, illiterate Styx.

Empire State's cool spire, clean as a snow-cap,
thrusts up its self-illuminated glory;
southward, there's Liberty, pistachio
and paranoid in her sleepless sunbeams,
interrogated nightly, not confessing.
It is not too dark to spy one sailboat,
pass by swiftly, lampless, veering westward;
one black-winged gull descending to water,
its quills immersed in the neon mirror.

Now it *is* dark. Now every shadow here
must warily watch for other shadows
(some come to touch, to be touched, but others --)
I stay until the sea-chill shrivels me,
past the endurance of parting lovers,
beyond the feral patience of the cat,
until all life on legs has crept away.

Still, I am not alone. The heavy books
I clasp together, mine and Edgar Poe's,
form a dissoluble bond between us.
Poe stood here and made a sunset midnight.
Poe cast his raven eyes into this flow
and uttered rhymes and oaths and promises.
One night, the river spurned his suicide.
One night, the river was black with tresses,
red with heart's blood, pearled with Virginia's eyes,
taking her under, casting him ashore.
One night, he heard an ululating sob
as the river whispered the secret name
by which its forgetful god shall know him,
his name in glory on the earth's last day.

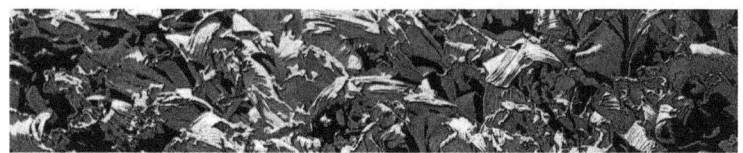

ANNIVERSARIUS XLIII: LET THEM PLAY!

"Mother, would you call the girls in? It will be dinner soon,"
Aunt Margie shouts from back in the kitchen.
I sit with my grandmother on the cool porch glider.
Across the street and on up the park's hill, her daughters climb
the steep sliding board and breeze down its shiny,
      polished curves.
Up again, downsliding, exulting the brief up-skirt blush,
legs not tiring, up again, down again, dolls put aside
in favor of the giddy height, the pull of gravity.
On a higher-up hillside, boys scale a tree, ride swing-sets
out and up almost to escape velocity. Ray guns
have replaced cap pistols, star-dreams of rockets in their heads.

My grandmother just smiles. "Oh, let them play!"
    she says to me.
"Another story I know, that I can tell you, aside
from the back-and-forth of the secret names of animals
(she never finished that one!) is why I say Let them play.
My mother told me true, one day in the clearing, *The day
will come when you have two, three, or half a dozen children,
and you will treat each one as a new-found jewel, a pearl,
a lump of gold. Then you will want to keep each one at home,
in sight, never to leave your guarding. I say Let them play!*

*Let them run in the woods. Let them chase and be chased.
Let them bite and be bitten. Let them climb up tree and rock,
wash their own little wounds in a clear, calm stream. Do not call
them until the last possible moment, till bread-crust cools
and the meat is singed black on the open fire. Let them play!*'

"Why, mother," I asked, 'should I let them run so late,
until it is so dark I can hardly see them coming?"

It happened, she said, *not here, but three villages
down creek and around the sharp-peaked mountain.
It was the time of harvest dance, a thank-you stomp to sun
and sky, just when all the trees had gone crisp and color-up,
a night when all the men would drum and dance on till midnight,
and songs would go on until it was too cold to sing
another, and the fires grew ashy and dim. With sweet fruit
and sassafras tea and honey, the children and their dolls
were sent to bed, tucked in and hugged, warned that the Wendigo
must not be permitted to see them. No child was to peek.
No child was allowed to stand in pretend-dancing that night.*

*In their longhouse beds, the children fidgeted, their blankets off,
their blankets on, as they heard the drum beats, the water-drums,
the shrill flutes, the deep-voice song of the men. One, whose name was
Not-For-You-To-Know, blew into a gourd and made sounds.
The women's chant answered, high and low. They all watched,
as those shimmering stars — the Seven —*
          what do you call them?" —

"The Pleiades, grandmother?" —

                    "Yes, the Pleiades!

"My mother called them something else, but she showed me
their glittering up-rise from the edge of the world. She told me:

*As the lonely, the desolate, the shimmering sisters crept
from the edge of the earth toward their place in the sky,
they could not harm the dancers – too far and too weak
in their sad darkness — but the children! Ah!* — she puts her hand
to her bosom and gasps, and pauses — "Mother!"
comes the call from Aunt Margie again. "Please call them in!"
Grandmother leans close to me and continues,
channeling again her own mother's speaking:

<17>

*But the children were not tired. Far from it. The song-dance twitched
in all their fingers and toes; their knees and elbows jabbed out
at one another in their beds. The straw ejected them.
They sat up. They crawled unseen into the dark-on-darkness.
In the shadow of the longhouse, no one could see them go.
And they began to dance! They danced! Up, knees! Down, feet!
The lonely spinster Pleiades, childless, saw them dancing.
They were light as feather-down, the children. They joined their hands.
All their feet went up at once. A little breeze lifted them.
The Pleiades with bird-claw fingers, lonely among stars,
ah! how they wanted to have their own sons and daughters! —*

"Mother! Do I have to go get them myself?
I know you're out there. I heard the glider squeak.
I hear the two of you talking!" Aunt Margie calls, close by
from the living room, the smell of apple pie-cinnamon
        wafting out to us.

"Not quite yet, daughter," my grandmother calls back
        assuringly.
"They're right where I can see them!" I look at her expectantly.
"And then? And then?" (Not another unfinished
        and interrupted tale!)

And then! she answers me, *while all the elders are thanking
the sun and the moon and all the good winds, thanking the Crow
for not taking more than his share, and the Bear for forbearing
to tear up the bark and logs of the longhouse —
a whole long, ancient list of Thanksgivings you can be sure —*

*the children are all trying to echo them, and just at
Crow-Thanks and Bear-Thanks, just when they hear
the elders address the Snow, that he should
not come too soon this winter nor stay on too long —
by then the Pleiades have got the children, the big ones
first, full of ten years, the not-so-big ones so full of corn
and six or seven years, even the sachem's dear son!,*

*even the tiny ones whose dance was no more than a stumble-
foot-stamp. All of them up! All of them higher than cornstalks,
higher than trees at the edge of the clearing. Fog-fingered
and jewel-eyed childless sisters of the cold space of night —
they took them screaming into the ink-black sky. Children, gone!*

*That is why their village was abandoned, empty. We passed
it with sadness and shuddering along the way. We wept:
their name was soon gone at the Council Fire.*
I look at her in disbelief. "I have said." she finishes.
"Mother!" Aunt Margie shouts; her face appears close-up
      behind the porch screen-door.

"Let them play, I say!" grandmother repeats. "Let them play
until they are so tired they drop to sleep! It is that time
of year. It is November and the night sky is lonely."

"Those stories again!" Aunt Margie complains.
    Her hands go up
as though to block her ears. "Why tell your grandson
    those stories?"

Grandmother stands. Her tiny profile and her jet black hair
defy her tall daughter. "I have said, or memory dies."

Soon the exhausted daughters are called inside to dinner.

Death and the Maiden

after the German of Matthias Claudius

The Maiden:
Pass me by, oh, pass me by!
Go, savage skeleton!
I am still young. Go, seducer,
and don't reach out for me!

Death:
Give me your hand,
    you delicate child.
My hand is friendly,
    not punishing.
I am not savage. Be brave!
These bony arms shall guard
your tender sleep.

The Place of Attics

Hard-rock New England
is a world of attic-dwellers:
spinsters and hermits,
bloodlines of schizophrenia,
tight-shut clapboards,
paint-peeled shutters,
a baleful eye behind
a soiled lace curtain.

Who passed the picket-fence
and glanced into the parlor
as Lizzie Borden
wiped clean the ax-edge,
returned to her bed
with a migraine?

Who idled in Salem
at the old spice shop
as Hester Prynne,
a half-moon frowning
upon her scarlet letter
took basket to market,
and who, averting her gaze,
passed by what locked door
to eavesdrop on Arthur Dimmesdale,
self-flogging, his blood beads
spelling the eternal A?
In Adams Fall, We Sinnèd All.

What batly belfry, bell-less
shadowed the wily minister
and his impish daughters,
as they bent pins for the witch-trial —
the spitting pins
they plan to blame on the innocent hag
whose farm and lands they covet?

From what high steeples
does what avenger look down
as the merchant's gold plate,
the fine furnishings,
the pastoral landscapes,
swell three floors high,
on gold from selling
rum to the Negroes,
molasses to the distillers,
slaves to the sugar planters?

What starry owl repines
beneath a rotting gable
to survey with unblinking eye
as the miser millionaire
shuffles by, slow-paced
in phlegmy wheeze,
walking a mile in old shoes
to find the cheapest chowder?

Does any widow's watch
stand guard at night
as trucks roll by,
as slit-eyed criminals
dump toxic waste
behind the schoolyard,
or a barge tips oily sludge
into the harbor?

Up on that mansard height
of City Hall, does even one
of those peregrine falcons
take count of a dollar's passage
from crack-smoke car-seat
to bicycle boy,
to the convenience store,
to basement warehouse,
to the unseen drug lord?

No Athens, Providence:
madhouse-state capital.
The roads are blocked.
Hotel rooms lock from the outside in.
Thieves smirk on the doorsteps;
they boast of useless crimes,
confess to hasty interments.
A tree-squirrel once heard one say
to his baseball-capped brother:
"I'm just going to rob and rob
   until someone stops me."

Nothing on high does anything.
The steeples jab Heaven's eye.
Monotonous, the bells ring on.
Men climb church walls on moonless nights
to steal the lightning rods,
the copper strips from roof to ground.
They'd scrape the gold-leaf halos
from off the painted saints if they could.
The sombre, brown, cathedral ceiling
looks like a never-cleaned toilet bowl.
Hordes hunch in rain each spring,
kneel in a shrine for guidance,
while priests' hands inch unseen
toward the choirboys' backsides.
Our Lady among the crawling rats,
tear-streaked in verdigris,
blesses all in diapason tone.

My neighbor, from rooftop eyrie
shouts out from his blackened windows:
"You're all going to die! All of you!
You're all going to die." Another night:
"I want a brain! I want a brain!"
he howls till squad cars' arrival,
then hurls his television to shards
on the sidewalk below.

On just my block, one attic dweller,
a landlady's schizophrenic son, hacks
endlessly in smoker's cough, tubercular;
another houses twin infants mongoloid;
another, a white-haired granny who thrusts
her head out, Medusa locks and all,
to scream at any long-haired man who passes.

I did not live in an attic there, the gods
be thanked, but I wrote in one.

ANNIVERSARIUS XLIV:
AT THE EDGE OF THE LAKE

Scorched by the blind frost, the maple leaves die,
and men who love not autumn herd them up,
with rake and barrel and ignominious shroud
of plastic trash bag. They are trucked to a fenced-in
municipal recycling center, a death camp, really,
bull-dozed and stripped of all identity,
chopped to mulch for next year's gardens.

Bird flocks rise up in arrow-shaped vectors,
riding the west winds out to escape us.
Leaves fall; *they* flee.

              While all this leaf-holocaust,
this flee-to-south abandonment
by nations of bird flocks goes on all day,
while long night chill crisps every lone cornstalk
and the dried-out irises droop, dying,
why are you doing nothing about it?

Abandon your sheltered room, I charge you:
gaze through the tree-bared acres at the line
of dark and leaden pines, black silhouettes
bold in the slanting dusk. A warning take
from the wind's disconsolate sigh; no hope
can they gain from the coming election.
Death weaves through the browning, rigid cat-tails.
Brittle they lean, seed-shorn and childless now
that the swamp has been drained; their realm will end
at a gravel barricade, a concrete wall
no seed can scale, nor root circumference.

The blasted oak tree wears its own dead leaves,
a bearded miser, while maple and birch
stand naked and appalled. Bulldozers wait,
silent steel mastodons at glacier's edge.
(There are plans, and trees are not part of them.
You and I are not part of them. A third
of the poor insects are already gone.)

From an old brick tower the carillon bells
play *Kommenoi Ostrow*, a plaintive song.
I go to the graveyard's shore of the lake.
I stand amid the blasted maples,
tree-fathers as old as any tombstone here.
A few yellow leaves I have rescued dance
around my feet in a sly dust-devil.
They will return with me to join
my curiosity cabinet
of well-preserved loves, and gelled high moments.

Autumn is not and never will be
an ending. Autumn piled up on itself
is a bottomless leaf-pile. Oh, plunge in!
Stand here still hearing the dying bell-tone,
as a wind that tasted tundra slaps
your face awake with icy needles.

Kammenoi Ostrow fades to silence.
Where does one make a stand for life?
There is nothing to the north of you,
and little cause to bird-flee southward.
This is the edge of the world.
This is where the first snow falls.

GETTING YOUR EYE

Your eyes eluded me again today.
Do not protest they looked for me
when I was not alert: my sole
intent was to discern
the hue of those haunted entrances
to your attention. I failed
again to catch them at home.

A momentary glimpse, between
a blink and a downward glance
showed a dark orb that flitted by,
a ghost traversing your cornea,
gone before I could capture it.
The appetizer came and went.
The main course was finished off
A costly dessert arrived. You smiled.
It slowly vanished in dainty bites
displaying your every perfect tooth.
I have memorized your ear-tracery.
I could draw your nose, the part
of your raven hair. But of the orbs
that guided the eating — *nada*.
Next time I shall come with a hypnotist,
a color chart, a spectrograph,
to map the shade and boundary
of your irises. That done,
I shall apply my finer arts
toward collecting the rest of you,
for there is a blank in my book
of love-spells that reads:
"Enter eye color here (Mandatory)."
Magic is unforgiving.

THE WITCHES
AND THE HIGH-COURT JUDGE

after Ben Jonson

WITCH 1
I have been all day looking after
a Funnel for His Fundament,
for he is like to Bouffe a Biere
as to pour it in his gullet.

WITCH 2
I have been gathering wolves' haires,
The madd dogges foames, and adders' eares,
to hie me to the Brewerie
and mix them in his favor'd Bieres.

WITCH 3
I last night lay all lone,
on the ground to hear the Mandrake groan,
and plucked him, to make a Dolle
that hath no Manhood on it, None at all.

WITCH 4
And I ha' been choosing out this Skull,
from Charnel Houses that were full
and I shall make a Lykeness Doll
that screameth, "I am a Man of Yale!"

WITCH 5
Under a cradle I did crepe
By day; and when the childe was a-sleepe,
I marked it with the will to tell
That he would four times eff with her anon.

WITCH 6
I had a dagger: what did I with that?
Killed an infant to have his fat.
I'll carve *his* name along the blade,
and hope he finds it, nick of time.

WITCH 7
A murderer, yonder, was hung in chaines;
The sun and the wind had shrunk his veins.
A strip of flesh I'll offer him up, a rag
from the convict to replace his robes.

WITCH 8
The screech-owl's eggs and the feathers black,
The blood of the frog and the bone in his back
I have been getting. We'll make him drink
ere that we walk him to the Devil's Train.

WITCH 9
And I have been plucking (plants among)
hemlock, henbane, adders-tongue.
If he be ever so fond of an Ale,
we shall wizen his innards, head to tail.

WITCH 10
I crept back in a house again, I killed
the black cat, and here is the brain.
Once he has tasted this, his memory
will never again be quite the same.

WITCH 11
I scratched out the eyes of the owl before;
I tore the bat's wing: what would you have more?
His robe will leap up, so he canna' see.
If Justice be blind, he blinded must be.

DAME
All, gather all, and bringe him hence.
With him bent o'er, we'll funnel him
all full of poppy and cypress juice.
All, add the ingredients, all.
There is a mile of intestines to fill.

And while we are here, let every orifice
serve as our Devil's Treize-Angle.
Into each ear a hornet's nest I'll stuff.
Here, sister, is dung well dried
that will cling to his nose-hairs petrified.

That termite nest, well-greas'd by Toads
will just about fill his booming maw.
What judgments he'll pass! What Odes
he will sing to his clerks and aides!
Not a word he says will be understood.

And as for that Implement he lov'd,
the Mighty Handful, Marriage-Plowe,
we'll wrap it now in briars. What fun
each time he looks in lust at a maid!

And last and most, ye Coven hags,
be comforted to know he loveth Biere.
Biere that every barmaid and man
shall be compelled to pisse-anoint,
Biere that shall bloat his ulcer-belly,
Biere that shall pass like vinegar a-boil
through his thorn-wrapped passage.

CHORUS
The four-times Eff that thou hast done
shall now be done to thee.

Thus Witches Twelve, unnamèd We,
shall run a Train on Thee.

The Cemetery at Eylau, 1807

The Battle at Eylau, East Prussia
 (now Bagrationovsky, Kaliningrad, Russia).
 As told to Victor Hugo by his uncle Louis-Joseph Hugo.

1.
Eylau, the graveyard in Kaliningrad, Eylau in East Prussia:
Eylau, the battle rather. Louis-Joseph was then
just Captain, and had earned the Cross, not that
it mattered in '07 when men in war were naught
but shadows and numbers to those who counted.
He would never forget Eylau, a quiet spot
(East Prussian then), mist-clotted fields,
scant woods. The regiment before a ruined wall,
an angry old belfry frowning down Lutherly,
gravestones one could not read, slabs a-crumble
and flat, sunken and swelling in humps of grass.

Beringssen, superstitious, shuddered to stay here,
but the Emperor would not retreat, not now, while
the threat of blizzard hunched in the clouds.
Napoléon himself went by, sunglassing the sky,
calling orders as he ant-scanned the horizon.
The word spread fast in spiderweb gossip, soldier-
to-soldier: "A battle, for certain, tomorrow."
They saw the shapes of women and children, fleeing,
huddled forms with knapsacks, potato-brown.
He looked along the ditches' edge, anxious to hear
the rumble of horses and wagons — but silence.

In the wall's shelter they made a campfire.
They made giant soldier-shadows, coming and going.
The colonel summoned him: "Hugo!" — "Present!" —
"How many men are with you here?" — "A hundred." —
"A plague! That's far too few. No matter then —
You take them all." — "Where, Colonel?" — "Go down *there*
and get yourselves all killed in the graveyard."
The captain laughed. "Down there! That is
 the very place to die."

He had a gourd, a decent wine. He drank.
He passed it to the discerning colonel,
who savored, nodded. Their eyes met. Each understood.

A chill breeze harrowed the empty branches.
"We're never far from Death," the Colonel conjectured,
"Much as I love my life." He raised the gourd again.
"Much as I love the *real*, we who know wine like this
know very well how to die." Grimly, he laughed,
then swept his hand over the graveyard slope.
"Yours is the point they will menace the most.
No matter the cost — hold on. The battle's real crux
is here." Climbing to the wall-top, he scanned the ground.
"Have you some dry straw, at least, for bedding?" —
    "None, sir." —
"Then on the ground it is." Soft graves, headstones,
a sunken spot or two, they'd find a way.
— "My soldiers can sleep no matter where," he boasted.
— "And how's your drummer-boy?" —
    "As brave as a rooster!" —

"That's good. So let him crow, and beat the charge
at odd times, day and night, run to and fro
so it sounds like an army is crowded in here." —
"Did you hear that, boy?" called Hugo. A tow-head raised
from a snow-bank and cried, "Yes, sir! Fear not!
I can make enough noise for a Roman legion!"

Taking him aside, the Colonel ordered:
"It is imperative you hold this graveyard
till six tomorrow evening. Hold ground,
be you alive or dead. And thus, farewell."
He gave a swift embrace and firm salute.

2.
Leaving behind the merry fire, they scaled
the crumbling wall to down-slope cemetery.
The old gravestones and their death-headed mounds
peaked with snow-clumps, rolled on and on like waves.
The snow was far deeper than they expected.
In tattered cloaks they sank to its chill-bed.
They slept well, as men of war learn slumber
without a thought of waking, or dying.

He woke at dawn. New snow had covered him
and made his lips icy. He sat up like a revenant
from the grave-mound he had chosen, poor *Johan H-*
who, dead, had no choice in the manner of bunking.
He was head-to-foot in a snowy shroud.
He stood up and shook it off, shivering.
A bullet breezed by his ear. "Ho!" he shouted.
"Lookout, what see you?" — "Nothing, sir! Nothing!"
"That nothing was no housefly. Sound the reveillée!"

Up popped the nine-and-ninety heads of men
from the Lutheran ground that had never seen
such an Easter rising. The sergeant called, "To arms!"
Red dawn was split in two by inky clouds,
a bloody-mouth leer at humanity,
sun-rise, Death-rise, the lamp of War. "To arms!"

For all the horn-call and drumming, the pots-
and-pans clamor of readiness, they in their turn
got only silence from the unseen enemy.
The shot he heard was but a random thing,
much like a ballroom orchestra player
who by chance picked up a horn and blew it.

Though blood was iced, they were warm for battle.
On the plains, the silent armies waited.
The graveyard-men were set as bait and lure,
on which the enemy might spend and waste.
They gathered along the protecting wall,
each one prepared to bleed for every foot deterred.

3.
And then it came on: six hundred field guns
roared their iron mouths, booming and thundering.
Lightning and fire-burst flashed from hill to hill.
Then Hugo's drummer beat the charge, in answer.
A colossus of trumpets answered back.
Down came the leaden shots upon the graves,
as if the very tombs were their targets.
Starlings and crows exploded in black clouds
from the shaken church's crumbling steeple.

One corpse but lately dead popped up half-height
as a mortar exploded his fine monument,
a preacher from the look of him, black-raimented
with a bony hand stretched out in admonition.
Skulls rolled through the snow like aimless billiards.

Then a day-defying darkness seized them.
Dawn would not give to day, the sun was shamed,
smoke rolled onto and up the slope, to wall,
o'er-reaching it, up to the church itself.
And then, in clot of gun-cloud came more snow,
a steady, head-pounding downfall of heaviness.
Soldiers against the wall were whitened ghosts,
others upon the ground a rose-burst of bleeding.
Down on the plain, fires rose from the smoke-sea —
villages now plundered were set a-light.
'til the whole horizon seemed one vast torch.

They stood against the wall, and they waited.
Till six o'clock tomorrow! the Colonel had said:
How could they make their shivering presence matter?
Not crouching this way like hares before a hunter!
"Morbleau!" said the lieutenant next to him,
"Our chance may come, and may come but once.
Let us advance *now* —" and then a bullet
ripped through his throat and he fell trembling, dead.

Napoléon, the Emperor, had set them here,
they knew not why, except to be a puppet show
of easy things to shoot at, a hundred armed men
pretending to be a thousand, by dint of din.
What would he tell the men? Their only goal
was to survive until a gold watch clicked on six.

He raised his sword, swinging it this way-that way.
"Courage!" he bellowed, choke-full of rage and manhood.
Out and apart from the others he stood.
He felt it not – not the thing that ripped him,
his hand limp, sword on the ground before him.
"No matter, for I have another hand," he laughed.
He used his good hand to shake the numb one,
counting fingers, all there, thanks be to God!
He took up the sword again. Soldiers' faces blurred;
some seemed to sink and falter. "Ah, my friends,
we have left hands for the Emperor, too!"

Too soon, the boy's drum-beating stopped. He found
the staggering drummer. "No time for fear!" —
"Six hours I've drummed. Six! I'm not afraid.
I'm *hungry*," the drummer boy protested.
The ground rose up — like an earthquake, it seemed —
the drummer was gone — Hugo's sword was gone.
A cry went up to heaven, coarse like crows:
Victoire, it cawed. *Victoire! Victoire! Victoire!*

"Let anyone who lives, stand up! Report!" —
The drummer stood. "I'm here. I didn't die!"
The sergeant from behind a tree: "I'm here!"
The Colonel rushed in on horseback, red sword
edged with the blood of retreating Russians.
He approached, saluted. "Who won the battle, sir?" —
"You did, you, Captain Hugo. How many still live?"
And Hugo answered, "Three!"

The Tea Party

New neighbor girls have settled in.
We hear the squeals and screams,
the mother-calls and father-scoldings,
through the open windows.
An angry hedge divides us in back,
though our houses lean together,
shingles and sagging porches
almost blending, identical
weeds abuzz with the same
busy-body bumblebees.

The low-slung church
of solemn Mennonites
sits glum and silent
across the street.
The girls' names are Faith and Abby,
ten and seven in stiff blue dresses.
Their parents seldom speak to us.

Just up the hill, behind a fence,
white-washed and cedar-lined,
Charlene and Marilyn,
   the Jewish girls
live in the great brick house
(anything brick
    is a mansion to us).
I play canasta with Marilyn (my age),
learn to admire her parents,
watch as they light
   the Hanukkah candles,
move among them summers
as hundreds congregate
at their swimming pool.
Their mother loves opera,
but not, she says,
not Wagner.

One August day,
an invitation comes,
crayon on tablet paper,
for tea with Faith and Abby.
My mother says, *Be nice and go.*

I sit in their yard
with toy furniture.
The doll whose daddy
I'm pretending to be
has one arm missing.

The tea, which is licorice
dissolved in warm water,
is served in tiny cups,
tarnished aluminum,
from a tiny aluminum teapot.
I want to gag
    from the taste of it,
but I sip on and ask for more.

Now Faith addresses me.
"I'll dress the baby
and we shall take her to church." —
"Oh, we don't go to church,"
I told my newfound Mrs.

"Never, ever?"
              "Not even once?" —
I shook my head —
"I've never set foot inside a church." —

"That's just what Daddy told us!"
Abby exclaimed. "You'll go to Hell!"

"You'll go to Hell and be damned!"
    the sisters chanted,
"You'll go to hell and be damned!"

"What else does your Daddy say?"
I asked them. — "He says
you'll go to Hell and be damned,
because you're atheists and heathens."

Faith looked fierce,
She poured more tea
and made me take it,
as if it were holy water,
as if I would drink
baptism by stealth.
She raised her cup daintily,
glanced and nodded
at the fence and the cedars.
My eyes followed.

"Charlene and Marilyn
will go to Hell, too,
right to the bottom
of the flaming pit,
because they're Jews
and murdered Jesus.

"Would you like ice cream now?"

First H.P. Lovecraft Waterfire, Providence

It was in his honor, really. The band,
by god, was actually from Yuggoth.
Upon the bright stage at Steeple Street, two
rugose cones were induced to shimmy-dance
as cowled Keziah looked on approvingly.
Most of the audience, unwashed
or overly manicured, jeaned or dolled-
up for later dates at the hookah-bar,
were quite oblivious to what or whom
the puppet orchestra gave its homage.

This was H.P. Lovecraft's first Waterfire,
art-sound-and-puppet spectacle amid
a river lit by flaming wood braziers,
as the hooded and torched participants
chanted a well-rehearsed chant to the Elder Gods,
seventy-two strong. Could Howard, misanthrope,
have ever imagined the echoing call
from bank and office tower, of words like
"Ia! Ia! Cthulhu fhtagn! Ia! Ia! Yog-Sothoth!"
or that a truck-size Cthulhu would barge up
the Providence River to the waiting cove?

One outraged preacher confronted the crowd:
"I rebuke you! I rebuke all of you
in the name of Jesus Christ!" And the band
played on, and the chanters chanted on,
and the stars sped on in their cold orbits,
and perhaps two lips, that smiled too seldom,
curled up and inward to a skull-teethed grin
somewhere in a grave along the Seekonk.

I tried to be a celebrant, really,
but repellent hordes of ordinaries
made walking on, unthinkable. Mothers
with babies. Multiple babies. Twin prams
the size of original Volkswagens
prevented my passage on the narrow,

cobbled walk. I tried. A great hound snarled, lunged,
and then, like the tricephalic hellhound
Cerberus, an apparition with three
leashed mastiffs confronted me. Then I whirled
into a noxious cloud of cigar smoke,
a toxic cloud and a man within it,
who would not let me pass. Backwards, sideways
I stepped then, as two autistic children,
one wrestled to fidgeting by his father,
the other hurling across the sidewalk,
thrust flailing limbs into my rib-cage.
I climbed a grassy slope to elude them,
looked down from afar. Most natives looked like
an undulation of stumbling spheres clad
in motley of random, unwashed laundry.

Then I came eye to eye with three young men,
(three dozen tattoos at least among them)
watching from the bed of a pickup truck,
smelling of gun oil, vomit and whiskey.
Binoculared, they eyed the Waterfire,
the celebratory burning braziers,
the fire-attendants' barge, the silent passing
of real and faux Venetian gondolas.
Have these men have ever heard of Lovecraft?

"Saw a boat with an octopus," one said.
"Yeah. Just flatboats with oars. The damn water
is only three feet deep 'less the tide's up."
"So jus' where the hell is the Hovercraft?"
the man with binoculars demanded.
"They said there was gonna be Hovercraft!"

I Dreamt I Was Dante

I dream in mezzanotte silver-gray,
donning the robes of aging Alighieri,
sandaled and aching with brittle legs,
heeding the call of Thanatos,
waking or sleeping?
I do not know! I feel the dew
as on my ankles, but these feet are numb,
the bony knobs and claws of an exile.
My limbs are brown and scourged
with years. An umber moon,
senile amid the drooling clouds, tilts
earthward and winks at me,
the knowing eye of eternity,
changeless and blistering.

A cypress grove, its rippled leaves
cat-furring the rigid columns of sky-
supporting trunks, the blue drear tears
of trees unbearable in daylight: how cool
they are, how wise reflecting in dew-cups
each one the tiny faces of moon and Venus
(so must we mortals, in mirror'd shields
look on the Gorgon face of Love!)

Among the trees, close-packed, I see a maze
formed by the slab-walls of quarry stone,
blocks of an unfinished temple to gods
whom the fall of an empire extinguished,
now a limestone catacomb roofed by a vault
of stars. The maze invites my errant feet
to tread its ever-regressive avenues.

At the far heart of the stone-cypress maze
in a niche cut out of purest marble,
on a pediment of onyx, Beatrice waits.
She is already dead, and I will die
before I can ever find her resting place.
That is the journey, and there is no Virgil,
and although I have read him, his silver lines
fade now to dust motes in my memory.

AT THE GRAVE OF HOMER

On Ios the itchy-haired boys,
picking at head-lice like monkeys,
hectored to death the dotard Homer
as he stumbled sea-ward, hands up
to catch sun's east-west wandering,
ears to the waves to ken the echoes
and tides that guided him daily
from arbor to sea-park and home
again. "Old Man," they taunted,
"You know the gods. What color
is the hair of Aphrodite? How tall
was Aias when he stood in armor?"

Calmly, he answered them: "Bright
as spun gold. Tall as a ten-year oak."

THE DOLL WITHOUT A FACE

Who is it who can tell me who I am? — King Lear

One tea-and-cookies Sunday, she had more time
to spend with me, the youngest son's first child.
As I sat, lap full of *Classic Comics*,
grandmother Rutherford rummaged away
in the unseen kitchen. "Where? Where?" she asked.
Wood drawers slid. Cabinets squeaked open.
"Ah! Don't slip away — I found it again."

She cleared the tea table. "More, please!" I asked,
and held the tea cup out. She poured, I poised
the full teacup and watched the pot vanish
onto a sideboard. Then she placed before me
a bag, soft, suede, as tan as the oak leaves
that still clung rabidly to trees outside.

It was tied with a leather cord, cram-full
of objects that tumbled out. Small things first:
shiny white shells, water-worn bright agates,
black arrowheads, a bronze scrap verdigris'd,
a miscellany of seeds and pods, dried
leaves and petals long past the hint of hue.

"It's like my rock collection!" I offered.
"Agates like *that* I get from Jacob's Creek."
She pushes that one aside, holds the black
arrowhead in the palm of her hand, "Sharp-
edged black glass, so good for arrows," she said.
"That's how my mother explained it." She traced
the edge along her cheek. I shuddered then,

"Be careful! Obsidian! Volcanic
glass. I find it in the road-fill. Aztecs
used it to cut out hearts. Sharp as a saw,
a surgeon's saw." — "You know too much for ten.
Your teachers don't understand you, I hear.
That's why I can say things no one should know
'til they are old, and writing, far away."

She reached into the bag, removed a doll,
an almost weightless thing of dried-out corn-husks.
It had a dress, blue-printed calico,
delicate red shoes, a beaded hat, braids
made of twisted corn-silk, blond white. Round head,
was pulled tight with cloth, but hard as a stone —
no eyes, no ears, no nose, no mouth, no name
one could call it, or any name one wished.

"Boy: these are the things my mother gave me."
She left a long pause for that to sink in.
"Things that my mother's mother gave to *her*.
The family called themselves the Whites. Took her
in, a young girl, Indian braids and all.
No one was who they said they were: Stouffel
White was Christoph Weiss in Germany.
Henry White, the son whose big farm it was,
he spoke English, German when he had to.
Lots of children, hands to work and pray with,
one more was easy to take in. A lot
of Mingos from here were going West,
Senecas too, driven from New York state.
Many who could pass, already had names
from husbands and fathers and from Bibles,
and settled out in the hills and hollows.
Some had their children taken out to school,
some women married whites who didn't want
an Indian man's children, so gave them up."

She went to the sideboard, a drawer pulled,
"Here" — a stern old woman in widow's black —
"is how she looked when she came back to us.
I never called her anything but 'Ma'";
she was 'Mrs. Trader' to the neighbors.
Ten years they had lived in Allegheny,
across the river from Pittsburgh, chairman
of some company board he was — died there
and she came on home. None of us did church
except for Christmas, and neither did she.

"You didn't talk about being a Mingo.
It was bad enough when the first war came
to say the good White name was really *Weiss*.
But then she just told everyone: not White,
not Weiss, she was Indian, plain and true.
We laughed. She tried to change her clothing then,
bought beads and buttons and Indian scarves.
My husband was furious. Our children
were called names and ridiculed, but then
a thing of shame became a thing of pride.
One day she sat on the front porch with me.
She had this brown bag and the things in it.

"*Sharp-edged black glass — this is good for arrows,*"
she told me, as one by one she brought out
the rocks, the shells, the copper shard, this flint
she said came all the way from Michigan.
This from our fathers' fathers, a bone thing
from a raccoon's private parts, and magic.
She had a name for each thing, and a place,
all in her mish-mash Mingo-Delaware.

"Then came this doll, this doll without a face.
I never saw her cry but once, and this
was it. She didn't let me pick it up,
just held it on her lap and said, "*Listen.
Remember. My mother gave me this doll
the day she left me at the White farmhouse.
She'd be gone a while, she said, and I*

*must look at her face, then at the doll's face,
then at her face and at the doll's again,
till when I saw its emptiness I saw
her grieved face, her deep black eyes, her forced smile.
'Just keep the doll with you till I return.'*

*The Whites were kind, and I worked hard.
Kept to myself and sang my own music.
When done with chores, and there were plenty,
I roamed in woods with the named animals
I knew from my mother's teachings. Three girls
I played with, not quite as sisters. They scorned
my poor clothing, my stubborn braids. Ma White
took all my clothes one night and gave me hand-
me-down dress and underclothes and new shoes.*

*I was less an outcast now. No Sunday
church for me, but we would play with our dolls.
Their dolls had porcelain faces, with bright eyes
and noses and ruby lips and blushes.
My doll — it had only my mother's face
that only I could see, and I just smiled
as happy with my little one, as they
with theirs. Summers I'd play apart, out past
the last corn-rows where the deep woods began.
Mrs. White called me in, but I wouldn't come.
I waited — one day each summer — she'd come.
A whippoorwill call in daytime, she'd come —
there'd be no embrace so wondrous, no eyes
so deep and dark and arrowed with sad tears,
nothing I wouldn't labor through so long
as she came with basket and moccasins,
dried fruit and candied ginger, a handful
of found rocks and feathers and those agates
that looked like sunset paintings done on stone.*

*Up and down and across three states she went.
The old trails ran north-south and west-to-east:
Salt Lick Path to Braddock's Camp; Braddock's Road
white-written over Nemacolin's Path.*

*She knew her way, scavenged and traded,
did God-knows-what to visit me each June.
Strawberry-time, I knew she'd be there
calling at the wood's edge for her daughter.*

*Three years it went that way. I grew. Sisters
and cousins of the Whites tormented me
for my strange ways, weird songs, and for the doll
that had no face. At night they'd turn it round
so that it wouldn't face the other dolls.
They said it gave their dolls bad dreams. I hid
it beneath my pillow, then in a box
where I feared it would suffocate. Ma White —*

*I could call her 'Ma' as long as the 'White'
was attached to it like an apology —
came back from town one day with a present.
A doll it was, a newer, cleaner, bright
of eye, five-fingered, five-toed, black-haired and
silver-shoed princess. She'd put to shame the dolls
my sisters had nearly wrecked with playing.*

*Soon I prevailed at a porch tea-party,
where my doll, 'Abigail' now reigned supreme.
White sisters scowled, knowing no comeuppance
could come their way before the Christmas tree
restocked their dolls with the latest fashions.
My doll was lecturing her inferiors
on the new rules of the White doll order
when, from the corner of my eye, I saw,
between two cautiously-parted branches
what might, just might, have been my mother's eyes.
I didn't turn to look. Girl-chatter blocked
the call of the day-time whippoorwill, once.
Maybe twice I heard it, but didn't go
to the wood's edge where I always met her.
Then she was there, in full sight, eyes all wide
in a wordless 'See me, daughter' greeting.*

And then. O my daughter, and then,
ashamed that my sisters might glimpse her,
sun-burnt and moccasin'd with her traders'
basket and pack — I turned back to my doll
and — I — pretended —not — to — see — her."

"This is how my mother lost her mother.
She never saw her again. In this bag
she hid away the doll, the arrowheads,
stones, feathers, dried blossoms and raccoon bones.
No longer could she see her mother's face
on the wrapped rock that was the corn-doll's head.

"She hid who she was, until the time of remembering."

The Sorcerer's Complaint

for Barbara A. Holland

There is no use deceiving her.
Her hooded eyes, in shadow, see
each shade and its dim penumbra.

Drinking *lapsang souchong*
tea at my Sixth Avenue loft,
she spies the nightshade, the wolfbane,
purpling the herbal window sill.

At pre-dawn hour when all others slumber,
she skulks by, just when my illegal pet
happens to dangle a tangible limb
out and then down the fire escape, three floors.
No one was meant to see that tentacle
as it lowered trash to the waiting can!

When she joins in my poetry circle,
my Siamese cat athwart her lap-book,
her balletic toe lifts up the carpet,
revealing last night's chalked-in Pentagram.
"Really!" she chides. "Demons don't answer calls
that easily, and I should know."

From sidewalk she called, "Are you on fire, or what?"
that night my more musty conjurations
failed to clear the chimney top and gasped
out every window of my loft.
"Nothing to see!" I shouted down at her,
"A meatloaf did not survive the oven!"

Somehow one shard of carbon-clot
detached and followed her, and stayed —
I let it, to punish her being so much
in the way of learning my business.

Yet she is obstinate. My tea and talk
are just too much to her liking, so back
she comes, her raccoon-collar coat turned up
against the cloud that hovers there,
on my command. Week after week,
that black and personal drizzle hounds
her Monday walks through Chelsea streets.

Umbrellas are of no avail;
they leak into her mouse-brown hair.
Wind blows the rain sideways at her
as she hurls herself among
bus shelters and doorway awnings.

There is no waiting out the storm.
The manual of sorcery explains:
it is easier to start bad weather,
than to stop it.

The Warning

I think the animals will come and live among us,
their habitats ruined, their forests burned, their seas
afloat with the litter-tide of our abominations.
It comes in small ways, foretold in dreams: the snake
amid the lettuce leaves: how does one eat
around its coiled length without disturbing it?
Is it a venomous one? — Will it take an egg
if I poise it at one end of the salad bowl,
and, swallowing it, slide off and ignore me?
Why, when I open my wardrobe door,
do two fawns stagger-stumble from it,
their deer-horse voices calling, "Hide us!"?
Why do I awaken, just half the bed my own,
the other half fur-snuggle full of breathing:
a great gray wolf, red-eyed and drooling?
"No need to worry," his bass voice assures me,
tongue lapping my hand 'twixt double dog fangs.
"As long as I'm here, the others will spare you."
"Others?" I ask. I sit up in bed and find
amid my clutter of chairs and Chinese, Egyptian
tchotchkes, blocking the view of Renaissance
boy (the enigma-smiling Bronzino print),
a diorama of wild animals on the move: bear cubs,
an eagle and a fox in tug-of-war fight
over a leftover steak from the refrigerator,
dark-mask raccoon faces, opossums peeping
from under the uplifted carpet's corner,
a raven (not stuffed, a living raven!) a-perch
my bust of Hermes. My foot, in search of slipper,
startles a whippoorwill that hoots at me.
A badger rejoins its den beneath my floorboards.
I am not their food and they are not mine,
but somehow, they will have to be provided for.
They are here for the duration, as the water rises,
the tornadoes whirl, the fracked earth shivers.
It is hard to look into their eyes without shame.

A Toast to Wendy

1.
Who fired the cannonball that this colonial manse
(now B&B a-host to poets!) caught up and lodged
in fireplace brickwork? The British, of course, from bay,
a frigate bearing down on Lafayette's abode.
This red frame barn of a house leans back in salt air,
sheds heat from six-paned windows against the blizzard
of modernity. Its literary pilgrims
arrive on the noon of New Year's Eve, their papers
bulging from backpacks, laptops, Dickensian journals.
They sign the open guest book: who sleeping with whom,
or chaste with Byronic doom-gloom, whose name is real
and whose pseudonymous, details of little note
as the house is all theirs. The rooms are all for them,
theirs the sole use the welcoming fire, the never-
exploding mortar of King George the Third inert
to even the most outrageous manifesto.

Off to their rooms they ascend on Escher staircase,
up front and down back amid the heaped-up bookshelves,
hostess-hoard of Brit-American volumes,
vestiges of her New York publishing career.
Like as not the bookshelves hold this place together
(Rhode Island shore a vast, connected termite nest
to hear the well-off exterminators tell it).
The walls bulge. Windows no longer square won't open,
pipes rattle and hiss, the wide-planked floorboards gap-toothed
beneath the cat-scratched and faded Persian carpets.

The stooping elder Anderson greets them; son James,
a new face to them, lugs bags and reminds them,
"Wendy will not be with us. She is gravely ill,
told us from hospital bed she wanted you here.
No matter what, she wanted the poets again."
Old Mr. Anderson seems dazed and disoriented.
He shuffles away as his son gives out advice
on local eateries. "Redleffsen's the best," James says.
He counts up heads for the morrow's breakfast, assures

them he knows his way around the dim-dark kitchen
that looms cool-cave behind the formal dining room.
"We'll get you breakfast, don't fear. My father's no help,
but Wendy made me promise to help you out."
To the one he thinks is their leader, James adds:
"Of course a large tip would be appreciated,
since I'm off to the ski slopes once this is over."

As midnight nighs, the fireplace sputters, poetry
sparks up and out, logs spurt out flame-salamanders,
to the lines of Thomas Hardy, to their Gothic
utterances, Poe-reimaginings, wild verse
salt-sown from Carthage in elephantine revenge,
Baudelairean bleedings, achings of heart-sweet
first love, oh what an overflow of unbashful
egos and peculiar tastes. James has joined in,
"I just want to listen," he says. So on they go.
But when one translates from Russian (Akhmatova)
and reads "I drink to our ruined house, *Ya pyu
Nad razorenni dom*, James interrupts them, "No!
That is just too close for comfort. Let's not say that."
So they veer away from Russian. The Hardy book
makes another round with its bittersweet savor.
The dining room clock then rattles out its midnight
clamor; before twelve-stroke fireworks erupt somewhere;
drunks who failed to kill deer fire off at the heavens.
They break out the champagne. Glasses are passed around,
and one spontaneously says, "Let's make a toast
to our absent hostess, a toast to Wendy!" "I'll join
in that," James answers, half-choking the words.
"A toast to our absent hostess! A Wendy toast!"

They drink, and being poets, they read some more, and more.
It goes on till nearly two, till one by one and
two by two they rise to go on up to their rooms.
"Listen!" James calls out to them. "I could not say it,
while you were reading and sharing your work with us.
But I can tell you now that Wendy — my mother —
she died at ten o'clock this morning. Her last wish
was that you all have your New Year's celebration."

2.
    Who slept, if at all?
Who lay awake
    and listened
as the bereft husband
in and out of knowing
roamed in his bedclothes
mouthing, *Wendy? Wendy?*
Then shaking his head,
You fool, she's dead.
Whose door squeaked open
to Mr. Anderson's plaintive
Wendy? Wendy?

Who listens as through
    the floorboards
James phones his girlfriend
    in Minnesota,
hears snatches of sentences:

"She was doing well,
brain-tumor surgery and all.
They planned to send her home,
but then the diabetes kicked in
and they had to amputate
    both legs."

    What walked just then,
        first up, then down
the crazy-angled staircase;
who thought he saw
    a foot, a knee,
    a calf, a thigh,
then rubbed his eyes
    of sleep-sand
and saw nothing?

"And so I came home. First time
    in a decade, to take my mom
to New York in her wheelchair.
Just one last time she wanted to see
the big tree at Rockefeller Center,
the lions at the Public Library,
the Bethesda Fountain."

    And who was it,
    in search of toilet,
    who saw and heard
     the pages turn
    in an open book,
    the Oxford dictionary
    on its oaken lectern,
    turn, turn, turn of page
    fast-furious,
    yet not a hint of draft?
    Who would not wish to know
    what word was sought
    and by whom or what?

"And then it got worse.
Back to the hospital.
They must have liked
her insurance policy.
This time they took her arms.
Both of them.
What was the point?
She died this morning."

    And who, in their bed
    where the Gothic dame
    and her platonic admirer
    shared one chaste mattress,
    reached out the hand
    that made her yell
        I told you not to touch me like that!
    And just as he protested
    That wasn't me!,

    what kicked him hard,
        rolled him clear off
            the bed to the floor?
    That wasn't me! she cried.

"My father. His mind is gone.
We were in the hearse.
Taking her, you know.
And he had agreed
 to God knows what,
signed up for 'the best'.
I lost it.
We have no money for that.
We had a screaming fight,
right in the hearse,
and so, it being a holiday and all,
we never —"

    What roamed the rooms
    so that every third book
    was pulled from its place
    and left at shelf-edge?
    The books, perhaps,
    she never got around
    to reading?

    What rattled pots
    in the kitchen
    in the pre-dawn hour?
    No, *that* was not a poltergeist:
    just the quarrelsome son
    and the still-angry father.

"There's nothing fresh!
No eggs! No milk!
How are we going to feed
these people?"

A car roars off. As poets stir,
it screeches back in.
Doors slam. A coffee smell
wafts up. Sun peeks
through clotted clouds,
frowning on Bristol
and its half-frozen bay.

3.
Sensing the rancor and chaos backstairs
two poets brave the kitchen.
They help, they set the table.
James does a yeoman's job of cooking
while Mr Anderson attends
   to a bin of dubious potatoes.
He wields a dull peeler
and just as well it is
they take it from him
and hide away the green potatoes
unfit for human eating.

Uncommon quiet rules the table.
Some make attempts to thank the Andersons
for hosting them despite calamity.
Each thing James says just makes it worse.
"You'll be the last guests we'll ever have,"
he tells them. My father is incompetent,"
he says while his father stands right beside him.

Breakfast has passed, and all have breakfasted.
Bags at the door, hugs all around, glances
at the parlor and its extinguished fireplace.
James looks at his watch, reminds them
of his urgent need for ski-lift fees. Wallets
and credit cards go and return.

At the door, he tells the last of them:
"Sorry I didn't tell you that my mother was dead.
And what I really didn't want to say at all,
while all of you sat eating there, and everything,
was that Wendy is in the freezer in the basement."

The Poet Who Starved

After Ludwig Uhland

Such was his lot — each dismal day
was short, and was marked with sorrow;
just as a poet ought, he withered
and quite forgotten, passed away.

He was an ill-starred infant
with only a muse hag for a nurse-maid,
and she it was who tutored him
to sing whether supper came or did not.

His mother, if one called some woman that,
crisped early to her untitled urn,
and so presaged his latter doom:
an anonymous and unread vessel
unfit for holding in or keeping gold.

When all around passed pewter mugs,
flagons and cups and champagne flutes,
he was the one they scorned to cheer,
pouring the dregs on cindered ground.

He knew the names of their fine vintages,
the lineage of kings who trod the valleys;
he could tell the rise and fall of empires,
but not one sip was given him!

Still, smiles returned to him each Spring,
his dreams of sweet blossoms woven,
but others hewed his trees to splinters,
boots muddying his purple stream.

When others orgied holidays, game days
and feasts, and marched in victory parades,
he raised his proud cup from afar —
his, the clear cold water; theirs, bloating beers.

The others watched him as he walked on by,
between his study and the library shelves,
thought him a pale being of scarcely flesh.
"He must have inherited money,

"an other-worldly man, almost a ghost.
He doesn't live like us. Ambrosia, mead,
strange fruits and berries, and a millet stew,
must be his monkish provender."

Dead! dead! they found him sitting there
over the crumbs of one last saltine, pot
of a weak tea too many times infused
until it was merely shaded water.

There was nothing in his house! Just papers piled!
Cupboards zig-zaggedy with spiderwebs,
ice-box unplugged, a gasless stove,
plates in the sink, oh, too far gone for mould!

Easy it was to carry him, pine box
weighing no more than pine box and a suit
of grave-clothes. No hearse for him: a handcart
sufficed to trundle him off to the graveyard.

His tread had scarcely marked the dust
when he walked of nights. May the earth
rest light on his shoulders. May someone find
those papers he left, and publish them.
May someone remember those words were his.

By a Roman Road Forgotten

Adapted from a Russian poem by Evgenii Yevtushenko

By a Roman road forgotten,
not far away from Damascus,
dead-faced mountains wear away
like masks of an ancient emperor.

Fat snakes that warm themselves
draw back their heads in coils,
bask their scales in the sunlight,
keeping their self-important secrets,
as if *they* had been with Cleopatra!

This was a road of damascene,
that rarest of steels for swords,
trade route for pearls and rubies,
rubbed clean by the bodies of slaves.

Legions marched in to invade,
profiles like Roman coins,
breast plates of bronze concealing
the venereal plagues of the armies.

Wheeled chariots once swayed
(before their wood was torn for cook-fire),
leaning beneath their drivers
like the crested coifs of empresses.

Laying the flagstones was the death
of slaves untold, each stone the back
of one fossilized workman,
an easy-ridden-over cenotaph.

Grown tired of his hot and Syrian exile
(too warm to even think in Latin),
the elegant patrician puts down
his lemon ice, to swab himself
in the finest Etruscan oil.

"Who cares if we crush this rabble
till nothing is left but skull and bones?
We Romans will not die like worms,
and the road will always save us."

Words not heard by the Arab mason,
dutifully pounding his hammer
to a slave-song obstinate,
a Syriac slave-song full of cunning.

"Thinking only about the flesh,
you have forgotten the gods.
Your death I hammer here,
and the road's death too."

Empire, decayed at the roots,
crept on, agape with gore;
veined, not like a tree,
but as a patchwork of blood.

Against resisters the Romans did
what they did best: the fire and tongs,
but torture victims sewn together
can only hold out so long.

The Romans took to sleeping naked,
their haughty togas put aside,
and so it was the Empire died,
and as well the ruined road I stand on.

They passed off their crimes to others
with the ease of the forger's art.
Some mile stones have only
the distant Emperor's name,
and some say nothing since
Diocletian had many worries,
least among them those awful Christians.
Who dies making the road is no one's
business. The road is not to blame.

But generations of wild grass
have had their way with it.
Only ghosts and goatherds walk
the dead *Strata Diocletiana*.
The road that engendered crime
Is now itself outlaw and criminal.

Let all the roads to executions,
and all the highways to tyrants' follies
come at the end to this ultimate payment:
forgotten, forever, in the highest weeds.

Damascus-Moscow 1967-68.

An Old Flame

On the eve of this dreaded holiday
I scanned the mailbox for pink fringes,
heart-shapes and scarlet arrows.

None, the gods be thanked.
I am well past pursuing, loth
to imagine myself the object
of any being's affections.

I glanced at internet beauty,
spectator sport. And look!
an urgent email
from someone who knew my name,
a mystery "old flame," he wrote me.
"How old?" I queried skeptically.
"You were my first," he teased back.

A date was made. The hour came,
and as expected, no one arrived.
I listened to Bach for an hour
then drifted off to sleep.

Sunrise on Valentine's Day
my eyes rolled open. Some-
one was in the bed with me.
We turned to face each other.

It was a Trilobite.

The Partisan's Woman

1.
There was a woman, wondrous fair,
and he loved her. She lived alone.
Her door was barred. Her lover last
had been a Partisan, and died
in the far-off mountains. No man
had seen her face, or touched her since.

He came to her door at sunrise,
bleeding. He knocked until a voice,
behind thick wood called out "Who's there?"—
"One who loves you still and always.
I have killed a man, and I bleed." —

"What kind of man have you killed, now?"—
"Policeman," he stammered. "My love,
I killed an officer of law." —
"Was he a bad officer, then?" —
"Like a wolf to the innocent." —
The bolts shot free. Just one pale hand
extended a clean, white bandage.
"Go and take care that no one sees you."

2.
There was a woman, wondrous fair,
And he loved her. One dusk, he knocked
until the soft voice called, "Who is it?" —
"One who loves you still and always.
I have freed ten men from prison.
Help we need to reach the border."
The bolts shot free. Both hands held out
a sack of bread and provisions.
She leaned forth and let him kiss her.
"Go and take care that no one sees you."

3.
There was a woman, wondrous fair,
and he loved her. Midnight, he knocked
until she stirred and asked, "Who is it?" —
"I who love you still and always.
I have brought you the tyrant's head."
Down he hurled it on her threshold.
The bolts shot free. Into her arms
the woman took him, laughing loud.
Goblets had she, and wine a-plenty.
"Love me," she said. "Love me from now
until the day they come for us."

4.
And the age of hard wars was long,
and the hunger consumed many.
The bees from the hive were absent,
and the dry nests fell from the trees.
Seas rose, storms fed the hurricanes.
Whirlwinds harrowed the empty fields.
Nights lay silent — crickets and frogs,
owls and nightingales on strike,
awaiting the high victory
of species, of each against each
and mankind against everything.

A hundred times the earth returned
to the place it thought it started.
There stood, in a leafless forest,
the partisan's woman's cottage,
a rotting skull upon its doorstep.
Nevermore did oak door open,
and nevermore were seen the man
or the woman wondrous and fair.

LOVE SONG IN FINLAND

after a poem by Goethe

How would it be if the dear one
came back exactly as he left me?
I'd kiss those lips so fast he'd stumble,
even if they gleam a wolf-blood red.
He would have to take back, too,
that cold formal handshake, heart-death
to me, that parted us. I'd press
those fingers even if they felt like snakes.
What is wind but words repeated,
tree to tree, from cliffs resounding,
losing meaning over ice floes?
Just so, the whispered promises
fade off when love is too long absent.
What would you have me renounce? Food?
I would shun all cakes and pastries;
I would refuse the monk's poor stew,
starving to win the beloved!
Whom once I charmed in fulgent June,
let him come, Winter-tamed, to stay.

FINNISCHE LIED (1810)

Johann Wolfgang von Goethe

Käm' der liebe Wohlbekannte,
Völlig so wie er geschieden:
Kuß erkläng' an seinen Lippen,
Hätt' auch Wolfsblut sie gerötet;
Ihm den Handschlag gäb' ich, wären
Seine Fingerspitzen Schlangen.

Wind! o hättest du Verständnis,
Wort' um Worte trügst du wechselnd,
Sollt auch einiges verhallen,
Zwischen zwei entfernten Liebchen.

Gern entbehrt' ich gute Bissen,
Priesters Tafelfleisch vergäß' ich
Eher, als dem Freund entsagen,
Den ich Sommers rasch bezwungen,
Winters langer Weis' bezähmte.

THROUGH MIRRORS

I play you through mirrors,
angled dreamt visions of you
I catch in candlelight

halfway across the crowd-cafe
you are fun-house warped to me
so close I can almost touch
each peach-fuzz hair on your cheek.

You are all there, from head
long-haired, form lithe of limb,
leaner than ever, as thin
as depth of glass. If I
touch this, will you yield
to my phantom?

I send a ghost-messenger
to follow your double home.
There you go. There, with you,
she (whatever she you deign
to possess this evening)
leans on your shoulder.

My mirror-self will follow.
When he returns
I'll reap the grief
of his report.

      Your kind
can only be wooed that way.
You do not see me looking,
longing. You lurk in corridors
of cold seduction,
between the mercury and glass

Only an Apple

after a poem by Plato

Melon ego. Ballei me philon de tis.
   All' epineudon,
   Xanthippe; kago kai dou marainómetha.

Look! I am only an apple.
Someone just fool enough
to love you, has thrown
me in your general direction.
Catch me, Xanthippe, now!
Tomorrow is too late for both of us:
a rotten fruit in a wrinkled hand.

WHY POETRY?

In memoriam: Annette Hayn

I see you always
in that photograph:
   a Breslau schoolgirl
   on a Sunday outing,
   resting
   beside a woodland path.
Everything is still before you:
in German Silesia,
   that 1930s forest
   where wolves
     and elf-kings peeping
   from the fern-fronds,
were the only things to fear.

Had you already read
the Schiller plays
   with their bold heroes
   and valiant women,
the Heine poems,
and the Goethe?

How far beyond those woods
were the Nazis waiting
   to deny you the right
   to your own German?

You sat in the audience
as Steinberg's hands waved
a brave Beethoven
from the *Kulturbund* orchestra,
until even Beethoven
was denied you.
The Jewish *Kulturbund* Orchestra
was banned from playing German music.

Later, the night-boat to England,
to boarding school,
away from the coming horror
   of Holocaust —
to America —
to marriage and children.

Something was missing
on those chamber-music afternoons
when your husband tore into
Brahms and Bartok,
excluding you —

no place to be
where the need for purpose
did not haunt you.

The business of the dead
   is to be remembered.
The business of survivors
   is to bear testimony:
But what is the business
   of those who *escaped*?

Find something,
   do something,
your husband urged you.
You had no cello,
   no violin —
only your hands,
   a pen,
     an ear for making word
     follow word,
tightrope-walking lines,
stanzas with their own
   bright magic.

You found it, finally.
Your world:
   surreally seen,
   Delilah and Noah's wife.
   much to do with doll houses,
   sailboats lost and found,
     the tracery of your children's
       lives and marriages,
and the friendships found
   among the poets.

You mined your own childhood, too
   and found it haunted
by the tread of history:
   your father in Breslau
    dreading the times to come,
   your mother skiing
     as though her life depended on it.

The places cannot be recovered:
   Breslau obliterated
     by the Red Army
and swallowed into Poland;
the Berlin of your schooldays
   a patchwork of memories,
your parents' names unwritten,
   fading from a whisper
     to the never-spoken,

but you found your truth at last
   in your poems and books,
where your escape
   bookended with silences
gifts us with thoughts
that will not perish.

The Warning of Solon the Athenian

Adapted from the Greek

Athanaia! Athanaia! Xaira Theá!

Athenians! We know that Zeus will never plan
    our destruction
nor will any of the immortal gods plot against us,
for such is the power of Wisdom, our great-hearted goddess
Athena, daughter of the king of gods,
she from whose bright temple extends her hands over all
who shelter in this blessed city.

But now her own people, for greed and profit,
risk ruining all, imperil the city itself with foolishness!
The leaders of the Assembly are of unsound mind:
bad morals and pride lead by the leash to a downfall.
Orgied, they know not how to restrain themselves,
or keep behind closed doors their gluttony and lust.
They have grown rich through bribes and malfeasance.
They loot the common land and temples, and steal
from the poor their tiny recompense. They scrawl
their one day's wishes on the tablets of law, rewrite
with their bloated thoughts the ways of our tradition.
The columns of Justice tremble but stand: does *She*
not know what is and was and has ever been?
Ah! she is silent, but for how long, Athenians?
How long until the truth avenges itself?

When corruption comes, the end is sure as disease
in wasting away the city: men's clouded reason
falls into an evil servitude, fathers and sons
brothers and sisters draw knives against one another
in civil discord and party strife. For no cause at all
except the desire to chaos, they bring us to War —

no matter the cause or pretext, a vile war does naught
but waste the prime and beauty of manhood,
leaving the polis a place of stumped cripples.

In their dark caucuses, yea, even in the Assembly,
they turn the ear to foreign conspirators; they turn
one faction of Athens against another, hating
their fellows more than the dread barbarians.
These evils seep down among the common folk,
those of little reason who but repeat the slogans
repeated o'er and o'er into their wearied brains.

How long will it be, if this goes on,
until our own citizens put on the chains of slavery?
How long until our own brothers are sent abroad
into strange servitude to masters we do not know?
How will we ever bring our kindred home
when their legs and minds are fettered thus?

And so the common evil comes to all, when flags
and bonnets and streaming slogans divide us,
house against house no longer neighbors at all.
Then come the evil officers with false arrest,
armed so that no door can bar their entry.
No matter what wall or hedge he leaps,
the single man cannot escape his judgment,
called before a dark and sinister tribunal.

So my heart bids me to tell you, Athens,
that even as bad government is as a pestilence
among us, good rule is like the cleansing breeze
that dissipates disease and ends disorder.
Wisdom shall hurl the evil-doers down
into the dark cells they have dug themselves
(all the cruel punishments their fevered minds
devised, not even those shall suffice to punish
the traitor who sells his own state to darkness!).

Wisdom shall smooth things out at the end,
if we choose her over hateful Eris, discord's
abominable mistress! She brings excess to order;
she stills the loud folly of bloated outrage.
No longer will weeds spring up in our roadways,
and once again will green abundance bless us
as all can walk freely without fear of slayers.

Wisdom shall straighten crooked judgments.
She tempers the pride of invention and wealth,
even the arrogance of the returning warrior.
The howling works of faction, the wrath of strife,
will gave way to common reason in the assembly.
Heed Athena, your only hope to make all good
and wise and perfect in the bright human world.

Athanaia! Athanaia! Xaira Theá!

(Based on Demosthenes, *On the Embassy*, in which the orator recites from memory these lines by Solon.)

The Rage of Athena at Troy

Adapted from Euripides' *The Trojan Women*

NARRATOR/PRIEST
Athena is wise, is wisdom, but beware her wrath: her name,
her rites, her honor must always be defended, her temple
sacrosanct. Hear her at the fall of Troy, when suddenly
she begs Poseidon to punish the Greeks, her favorites:

POSEIDON
[Welcome, Athena! *(Ironically)* Family love has a magic power.
...
I suppose you bring some word from Zeus.

ATHENA
No. I come to entreat your power, aid and alliance
on behalf of Troy — yes, of this place!

POSEIDON
Have you renounced your hatred? Now that it stinks in ashes,
do you pity Troy?

ATHENA
                Will you support me?

POSEIDON
Tell me your mind.
(Suspiciously). Is it Greece ... or Troy ... you are helping?

ATHENA
I am disposed to favor the Trojans, whom I once loathed.
The Greeks are leaving, laden with wealth and women —
make this homeward voyage disastrous for them.

POSEIDON
Why this leaping at random between love and hate?

ATHENA
You know of the insult offered my temple at Troy?

POSEIDON
(Places fingers to forehead, seeing a vision)
Ah! my eyes see it. Ajax athwart the door of your temple.
He is in! He drags a Trojan princess by the hair.
He has torn her from your altar, her offering
still fresh, a heifer unmurdered, a costly robe
upon the knees of your statue. It was —

ATHENA
Cassandra! The self-doomed Prophetess
who threw herself on the mercy of the gods.
He seized her from the sanctuary!

POSEIDON
The Greeks have spoils enough. Are they not shamed?
Must they not return her, that she complete
her sacrifice, her plea for safety beneath your wings?

ATHENA
They have done nothing. No punishment for Ajax,
not even a reprimand. The insult!

POSEIDON
And you, Athena, fought beside them. You rode
the war chariot with Diomedes, you felled
your brother Ares in a single blow!

ATHENA
Help me now to make them suffer.

POSEIDON
(Nods his head in assent, extends his hand).
My powers await your whim, Athena. What shall we do?

ATHENA
I mean to make their homeward journey a long one.
They will part from one another. The sea
will be their undoing, their misery.
Many will wish they had died at Troy.

POSEIDON
(Excitedly). The whole Aegean I'll stir for you; the shores
of Mykonos, Skyros, Lemnos, the reefs of Delos,
the Capherian capes I'll drape with drowned Greeks.
Go back to Olympus and get your father's thunderbolts.
You'll need them. No punishment is strong enough
for those who profane the temples of the high gods.

CHORUS
Athanaia! Athanaia! Xaira Theá!

This excerpt was included in the 2008 pageant-play, *Who Is Athena?* performed at The Providence Athenaeum on July 11, 2008.

Writer's Block

for Barbara A. Holland

Figure of speech
   this is not:
the black monolith
before your door —
so tight a visitor
or the timid mailman
can just squeeze past it
into your vestibule —
is real, and solid.

This object, taller now
than a double-decker bus,
is clearly out of hand.
Just when the charcoal monolith
popped up in the gutter
   like fungus
is not so important as how
it grew at curbside,
consuming a parking space,
   a bus stop,
cracking the Plexiglas shelter
until the smooth black slab
   jostled a tree
   and warped the sidewalk,
flush to the bottom step
of your brownstone front!

What is it made of? List all
the known black stones: basalt,
ebony, onyx, obsidian,
lava, jet, or hematite.
No match. Nor is it coal,
charcoal, or carborundum.
It is more like a cenotaph
carved out of frozen shadows.

Who knows where it
   gets its strength?
(Taproots in powerlines,
perhaps, or steampipes,
or gas and water mains?)
Does moonlight feed its
   blackness?

It festers there,
   absorbing sunlight
   like a cubist tarantula,
its height advancing
   in bamboo stealth
to the edge of your curtains,
an anxious bird perch
that finally shoots
   to rooftop,
five stories now! Five,
and it does not topple!

Up there, your morning view
must be night, now —
a blank night
without a hint of aurora.
Your darkened rooms
hunch in resentment.
The potted palm
   yellows and dries,
your windowsill
   a hecatomb of withered flowers.

And all the while
   your computer dims out,
   that manual typewriter
   from your student days
   refuses a carriage return,

your fountain pen is clogged,
pencils worn to useless stumps,
as a parallel mountain
   of crumpled paper
   accumulates.

Your poems germinate
   in beansprout lines,
but the stanzas coagulate
   into thought-clot,
   as useless as
   a castaway scab.

2
This state of things
   will never do!
I know a consulting shaman
adept at elementals.
He begs for quarters
at the corner of Morton
where it meets Hudson Street.
If you but ask,
he'll circle your house
with Indian maize
(to the delight of pigeons),
hang a dented silver spoon
on your fireplace mantel.
Then, after a swig
of a sassafras philtre,
his gap-tooth mouth
will eject dandelion puffs
and the scent of burnt sage;
on fire, he'll pull the tail
   of the Wendigo,
enraging his northern eminence
until its four crossed winds,
its burning feet of fire
converge at the pinch point,
galing down the Hudson River,
huffing from the piers

to your doorstep,
pounding that monolith
flat as a paving stone.
Like melting ice
   it will merge with the sidewalk.

He's done this for others —
but something is always
left behind:
that's why,
   at certain corners,
dust devils harry pedestrians
tornado leaves and paper scraps,
raise skirts and strip
the skins off frail umbrellas.

The shaman's fee for poets,
since we have less than he has,
is but a cup of coffee
and the promise of an epigraph.
Some lingering vectors
of anarchic wind
are but a small aftermath
of old-fashioned magic.
Lady, the bum's coffee
at the corner diner is but
a paltry ransom,
for imprisoned sunlight,
fettered typing,
   and a hostage pen.

Out-Home Summers

1.
"You'll eat those words."
We did: they sprang from the dirt,
ringed in the hearts of tomatoes,
bad news and outrageous claims
for miracle cures, crosswords
and obits ground up in pulp;

words we put in the ground
with the tomato starters —
on hands and knees in the garden,
we wrapped the roots
in old newspapers,
a wood-pulp wall
against the hungry worms.

Grandmother explained:
by the time worms ate
through the paper, the plants
were tall and sturdy.

At night I wondered
if the root-hairs read
about Russia and fallout
before they sucked
the paper dry
of lampblack ink,

whether the red fruit cared
which party came to power,
or how tomato-red was a color
to call someone a traitor with;

whether we are what we eat
as last season's news fades,
yet stays in our genes,
bone marrow memory of words.

2.
One time only I watched
grandmother kill off
an unruly rooster.
Over the executioner's stump
her hatchet rose and fell,
one deft and practiced chop.
The hated rooster's head
lay there on tree rings
in a red pool, while
the rest of the bird
made tracks for the forest,
blood jetting in air.
The dog ran after, gleefully.

I looked down at the rooster's
baleful, taciturn eye.
Did he regret now
the vicious leg-pecking
that led to his demise?
Did he disdain the race
the rest of him was having now,
in which the dog would surely
   triumph?
The open-beaked, expressionless
head just lay on the block,
as dignified as any isolated
head, as if to take root.

The dog retrieved
the exhausted victim,
now off to the plucking.

Each hour I came back
from the defeathering orgy,
the gutting and cleaning,
to the discarded head.
What was it thinking?
What was it thinking?
It must be thinking something!

3.
In early summer wood,
May apples pepper
the pine grove floor.
Copperhead snakes flee
my grandmother's
all-purpose poking and walking stick,
same stick that finds mushrooms,
morels, the best ones,
wherever they hide.

Pine's lower branch
drapes lawn,
trees hung
with bygone nests,
eggshell debris.

The black
snake molts,
counting the days
until re-birth and eggs.

Gone now three years,
grandmother returns:

I tear her from earth,
wipe off the sod,
know her face, graven
in May apple, mandrake root

4.
Red sky
that summer of twisters,
and of Hurricane Hazel,
sent everyone down
to cellar-holes,

everyone, that is,
except our heathen family,
storm-loving Odin's kin.
We watched
tornado pitch
rip arms
off poplar men,

heard not the song
the religious sang below
to bring their god down,
to spare their cars and rooftops.

Safely on screened-in porch
as lightning jabbed everywhere
I made up my own
ascent into sky,
waited for wind
to peel the house
like an onion.

We were sad when the storm
ended. Everything else
was anticlimax. No one
we knew was carried off
into the funnel's mouth.

Still, we would never forget
the wild song of the winds howling.

5.
Grandfather never worked a day
in all the years I knew him.
Content in his tar-papered house,
he sat in his long underwear —
what use to dress except for company?

But when the tax-day came,
he went to the mines,
spat at the very mention of them,
shamed
if one of his grown sons joined in
to help their Pa pay the property tax.
"I don't want you going down there,"
he told his son. "No man should have to,
unless it's that or starving.
I wish I had back the years I went there."

Without a nickel between them, then,
they'd hitch a ride to the Hecla mine,
grim-jawed at the thought that earth
might swallow them each time they dropped
into the maw of darkness.

They left before dawn,
returned in time
to watch the darkening sky
spit diamonds.

They hung their carbide lamps
by the wash basin,
the musty smell
of acetylene mingled
with soap.

The tax bill paid, his son
would return to his paper mill
up North. Grandfather went back
to his radio, weeks in long underwear,
the day-count to the welfare check.

Inside him,
where the coughing had
already started,

a hardened vein
of dark dust and tar
exploded one night
and killed him,

as he always knew it would.

WHO CARES TO LISTEN TO SONGS?

Translated from the Russian of Anna Akhmatova

Who cares to listen to songs
now that the prophecy of bitter days is true?
Hear me, old songs: the world has ceased
    its being marvelous.
So hush, and do not break my heart.

Like swallows, not long ago
you led the morning out, ignoring its risks.
Now songs like this must lead a desperate life,
begging for crumbs at strangers' doors.

A Haight-Ashbury Autumn

I must sing of the void.
Cacophony I chant,
and the gray sombre Chaos
of October.
Unfolding days in the twilight of equinox:
    chill morning fog and dew,
    sleeping-bag runaways
    stirring for incense and donuts.
I miss my Appalachian Fall
    with its red and yellow blaze:
This is Haight Street
      in western autumn
  where no leaves
  aggregate orange
  rust the earth,
  just brown and grey,
    a pitiful deciduous
    protest against sun-slant.
No leaf-piles are here to play in,
for down past Stanyan
    in Golden Gate Park,
citymen cart them away
  to great white incinerators.

I walk the park woods at night
yearning for the crisp of maple,
the underfoot carpet. Musk smell
and eucalyptus mock me.

Above, a meteor winks:
a falling star attains its own glory
in leaf-drop immolation.
Gone, yes,   but it was *up there!*

1967, rev. 2019

The Plasma Physicist Explains

If you want to understand me,
it's all in the science, really.
I am not like men.
I am not like women.
I am not an animal at all.
I am the fourth state of matter.

The soul of me
is a plasma core,
my heat contained
in vacuum walls
no cry can penetrate.

Swift currents and fields
hold me in check.
My delicate bell
of unprotected truths
must not be touched,

for I am lethal:
I have the sun's
incarnate eye chained here.
It is all I can do
to hold it in.

Come not too close.
Do not inquire
what burns within.
I have coped too long
with the break of heart
to need a supplement
to my magnetic fields.
Though I bulge out
ionosphere coronas,
and Northern Lights splay
through the bullet holes
of once-attempted affections,

my furies are self-contained.
A detonation was imminent
when someone came too close,
but one look at my lightning
is usually enough of a warning.

Orbit me at a safe distance.
Be warmed by what I generate.
If space and speech
did not restrain your hand,
if any speck of you leapt to my heart
it would become a barren nucleus
chained like the rest of me
into this welded egg of fire.

No need to feel sorry.
I am fine in here. I will last
as long as sunlight, till gravity
calls everything home to null.

On Rhyming Poetry

A parody of Barbara Holland's "Black Sabbat",
upon the occasion of being forced
to listen to doggerel

Thou shalt not suffer a rhyme
   to live;
thou shalt not suffer a rhyme.

for rhymes are tedious
merely in their existence.

Four hundred years ago you
   bored us on the page,
now in this steel-stitched century
   you tease us!

Often I have been aware of you,
of your comings and goings
   at the end of the line,
but it was not until I saw
   the pack of you,
a word-snarl of mouthing lips,
bloated with overscanning,
count-fingering, thumbs in the heart
   of a rhyming dictionary —
drinking the blood of a line
   that was good by accident
in the gray wet light of high school ...

until I saw you fawning before
   that goat-headed one
to whom you pledged Art
   on pain of strangulation —

Desist! No more. Some poems
may walk the railroad track of verse,
but do not call your hammered-rhyming
thing a Poem. Begone, gadfly! Shut up,
you sledgehammer-pile-driving woodpecker!

WOTAN MEETS SIEGFRIED

You, Wanderer,
   graybeard and granite-skinned,
    obdurate in wind, leaning
    upon an ancient staff:
what storm
   brews now inside
    those stony silences?
You loved
   a woman once, a son
   sprung from her easily —
through him, a son again.
Is that the boy,
   now climbing the crag
   to goat heights,
   his golden locks
   a laugh
    at your receding gray?
Who are you,
   anyway, the stripling asks,
under that hat?
Why is its brim so wide,
why does it droop
across your face like that?
You answer
   uneasily, *It is the way*
of travelers to bend
a hat against the wind.
He spies
   your missing eye,
   your need to defend
   a sightless side.
   Somebody else whose way
   you blocked, no doubt
   he plucked that eye out?

Taunting,
   the young man edges
   to pass,

      barred by
    your swifter arm,
    your staff of ash.

You know him now:
    Siegfried, son of Sigmund.
    You say: *The eye I lost*
is one of the ones you use
to see the one I have left.

He is not much for riddles.
Lunging, he breaks your staff.
He pushes you aside
like an inconvenient boulder.

You have nothing to tell him
he cares to hear about.
Like father, like son:
even with ravens to help,
you never saw anything coming, either.
Entropy scorns the immortal.

AT THE TOP OF THE WORLD

Is the mountain the object of climbing?
Does the act of climbing alone suffice?
I say: To climb is to achieve that height
    from which, alone,
you can scan the overarching beauty
of a curved horizon filled with summits.
It is not the triumph of reaching top,
but the sudden and dizzying knowledge
that what you scale is but a single hair
on the bristled, old beard of the cosmos.

See now the range of upthrust pyramids
on which you perch, a height-giddy rider
on the hump of a thousand-mile camel,
a speck on the Andes' anaconda.
Blue peaks, pure snow, kingdom-encompassing
rainbows, stark shadows cast as lambent sun
inks fold on fold of airbrush shading
upon the distant ranks of staggered hills —
all this you spy, and make out something more:

upon each mountaintop
    is the form of yet another climber,
your brother who stands and regards you,
      eye-to-eye your equal.
Or sometimes, in a condor solitude,
you find the driven spike and banner-mark
left by a climber who has come and gone.

Sometimes a scaled peak is vacant, but, lo!
Take hold the rock and gaze down vertiginous,
and see that a figure is scaling upward towards you.

Is it the same for all who struggle
    out of the shadows into the sun?

You cannot turn back. You belong no more
    to the towns and folk of the settled valleys,
where they see only your shadow pass,
    and fear it: to them
you are a spectre now, a name
    that induces a shudder.

Down there, they hone
    their knives and swords,
covet, enclose their neighbors' fields.
Their cannons spark —
    this way — that way —
in the depths of distant gorges,
their bloated and river-hugging cities
engulfed in flames
as each invades the other.

Could you go down and tell them?
Could you stop carnage they so revel in?
No! Thin air and star-glory,
    cloud-food and fog
are now your homeland,
    a cold rock your throne.

On what goes on below,
crusaders on horseback,
earth-drilling rape of the mantle,
the belching sulfurous hell-fires,
the gods and their mountains
look down in scorn.

The Autumn Fungus

The autumn is full of spores.
They make me forget
bad food, asbestos air,
the unburied corpses
upon the battlefield.
Their mushroom heads
pop up like babies,
their fruiting bodies
fragrant and sensual.

Chilled now,
the brown-and-purple *fuligo*
no longer creeps
from its fixed place
at rotting tree-root,

but elegant umbrellas,
gray and brown and red-capped
form their own marching line
along the tracery of root-rot,
athwart the squirrel's
doomed acorn burials.

Shelf fungus drills
into the anguished bark
of the street's last-standing
copper beech patriarch.

My keen ears make out
the chitter-chit of termites,
the acid-song of carpenter ants,
running a food-race
with their fungal cousins;

my eyes are keen enough to see
that even mushrooms have their mold
inhabitants, a fringe
of Richard-Nixon five-o'clock
shadow lining their edges,
black aspergillis, the rot
that dares not speak its name.

Mycophiles' delight? The feast
of insects, faery furniture?
I am in no hurry to dine
on any of my chlorophyll-free
kindred. Too soon, I know
their business will be
the digestion of me.

Congress, in Recess

Reform, like
Zeno's arrow,
never comes:
before the halfway measure
must come the quarter measure,
before that,
the hemi-demi-semi measure,
before that, the intention,
never mind the will.

Lacking the single push of empathy,
the bowstring is unreleased;
indeed, it was never pulled —
the fat hand, weighted
with golden rings,
the bribed wrist,
the obligated arm
the withered loins
Medusa-paralyzed.

Fear no arrows from this
sclerotic body.
Congress is in recess.
Congress has been in recess
for longer than anyone
can count.

THE VIRGIN MARY, AFTER ONE VIEW OF THE KAMA SUTRA

after the painting by Campin

Flemish Maria has been up all night
reading the sweet books her lover procured,
unruly books with their naughty pictures
of men, and of maids, and of beasts and bees,
verdigris-colored lawns and turquoise skies.
Her nurse concealed them in sewing basket
past the ever-watchful eyes of parents.

She's read all night, and studied positions
shown in an otherwise unreadable
quarto that Jan procured from India
(he would explain *everything*, he told her).

Now night's dim candle has been extinguished
to barter for study in morning's rays.
Another book, the holy one, adorns
the tabletop, but *hers*, she must conceal
by veiling its more lurid reds in silk.
She dreams of a Bengali gazebo,
how two bronze-banded arms might hold her tight.
Two other men watch through a latticework,
chestnut-brown eyes upon her nakedness
while she pretends to be none the wiser:
O Eros, what a great game thou playest!

To catch the light she kneels; her elbow leans
on velvet cushioning, quite unaware
of how the in-folds and out-turns of gown
have lured two peeping, immaterial ghosts.
First, Gabriel: a beardless, mincing boy,
a wingèd beauty, but no match for her.
Heaven's eunuch flaps in like a sparrow
for a chat with the studious maiden.

He tells her what God has in mind. — "Why me?"
She can't imagine why she was chosen.
Her protests will not help — though she is not
a virgin, really — she has promised, sworn
to run off with her gentle ravisher.

"His name is Jan. He is not remotely
angelic. Odd teeth and a broken nose.
Why not choose that blond, Angelica, who
all but asks for it with her haughty name?"

But the angel babbles on about it —
his speech was all memorized, anyway.
He says she'll be an unwitting mother,
warm hen to an invisible rooster,
then, a mother of one whose destiny
was written in stars and a prophecy.

"No, no," she says, "I want no part of this,
Jan would never forgive me; how could
he raise a son he did not recognize?"
Down comes Maria's second visitor.
This one does not negotiate consent:
the ghost streaks down like molten mercury,
the tiny cross he rides like arrow-bolt,
aimed straight at her womb, a battering ram.

This missile is Christ in miniature,
prefigured end already there in seed;
for her, a birth unasked-for, All-Mother-
of-Dead-Son her immortal agony.

Her eyes turn again to the outlawed book.
If she pretends she never heard the angel,
that nothing but a gadfly descended,
that a picture is worth a thousand words
of that indecipherable Sanksrit —
She sighs and thinks: That's Jan on top, and me
on the bottom. Those chestnut eyes behind
the open latticework: watch over us!

The Return of Richard Nixon

Confront them. Wing them away
in a one-way helicopter.
Damn it if they don't come back
like termites or carpenter ants!

After a "decent interval"
the scoundrel Nixon came back.
He was on the best-seller list,
dashing about the talk shows,
a flutter of paper wings
on a rumpled dark suit.

He mingled among diplomats,
pressed hands of potentates,
showed teeth
behind the wrinkled dough
of a smile,

his head-on gaze at the cameras
said, "You see, I am not crazy.
I could have pushed that button.
But I didn't."
He fund-raised for candidates.
He stood in the reception line
and people told their children
as though they had met a Borgia,
some Pharaoh of Egypt,
or the dreaded Torquemada,
and lived to tell the tale.

The mirror
made no mistake.
The only reflection he had,
like an old cloth coat,
told him that skin was hard,
stayed where it was pulled,
that blood coagulated,
vision receded, friends

said they would call
but did not. He heard,
when he walked the golf course,
the mocking caddies parroting
"Not a crook. Not a crook.
Not a crook."

Still, there was talk,
when he rose each day
and put on the requisite tie
and the American-flag pin.
Some said he wasn't too old to serve.
The ink of the pardon was dry.
People just don't remember.
They liked him in China.

I shuddered each time
I saw his face on the news,
and I called out in anger:
America,
don't give a snake
a leg to stand on.

Moving Day

Sometimes it takes a farewell
to get the earth to yield its promises.
Say an *adieu* to barren trees,
pack your belongings up in trunks
and packages — and then it starts.
A house in a better neighborhood
no sooner leased than a sun
rekindles every root with nascent spring —

the pigeons hop in mating dance
as if their talons burned from it;
squirrels unfold their nests of leaves
and clamber down to forage seeds;
and through the vast transparency
of paths I see again
the smooth white legs of runners
outdistancing the Spring.

And yet it's always so.
I move to a place because I think
I will love it, but then I know
I am mistaken. Trees fall,
friends die, the loved do not
love back sufficiently.
I choose a new place because I think
I will love it, but then I know
that age and entropy are the same
everywhere. Too-many-times-
moved ends in plain-sight invisibility.
This time it may be the end of me.

Look at those crocuses, those gold-
tipped stalks intent on daffodiling!
Witch-hazel, forsythia, cornelian cherry
teasing with early blossoms!
Windows thrown open, faces
beautiful to behold regard me.
A passing cars's boom stereo

plays Mahler's Second Symphony
as it dopplers on by. But here it is:
the moving truck arrives. Boxes
encase my every breathing word.
The books have gone to sleep,
all nestled dark with their brethren.
The kitchen is disassembled,
recipes entombed, spices sealed up
in their canopic jars. The pots
and pans are free to clatter
as the truck weaves and sways.

Why is the old place so beautiful now?
It is always thus:
When Love must yield
to parting words, she
turns her fairest cheek to kiss.

Life Without Siegfried

Thoughts while hearing Georg Solti and The Chicago Symphony perform Act III of Wagner's Götterdämmerung *in concert*

1.
Here walks young Siegfried by the Rhine,
armed with a Ring the old gods lost,
curled in a fist, that ancient gold,
its sun-gut power crushed to grams
of portable might.   This hero, half-awake,
does not yet know himself.
He has lived among bears and evil dwarfs.
He knows not what power means,
nor in his brazen youth believes
the Rheingold curse's warning.
As the nixies taunt him, he almost hurls
the thing into the river — let them have it;
it's neither good for food or fighting —
but he yields instead, self-irked
to danger's lure — his strong arms
enjoy a good battle. He savors fear
as though its loss would soften him.
He will keep the Ring, to see what happens.

Already you are drugged, young man:
the Tarnhelm poison pours mercury
across your eyes, blinds you to envy
and to those who tread along behind you.
You love the hunt, the running ardent life;
sun-gilded trinkets are nothing to you
since you eat from the nut-trees and hunt-fire.
You are proud of your strength, your certitude
oblivious to oaths of greed and lust,
the lure of pleasure that ends with knife-thrust.

As music soars, some listeners both hear
and see. Others have obsidian, dead eyes,
inverted smiles frozen in Republican hauteur,
Mrs. and Mr. Gibichung in furs and wingtips.
She has done nothing to harm anyone.
He has perhaps done a great deal to a great many.
The thin and tender line between cynic
and murderer: one says no heroes live;
the others makes sure all heroes are killed.

This opera is not for its audience. It dwells
in a realm of ideas, forms crystallized
in words sung, spun upon leitmotifs
that make all words much more than their sum.
Siegfried, you do not know
you are being played through, lived through,
a thousand voyeurs and auditors engaged
in your triumph and love and loss.

At the last, pathetic youth,
when your eyes are cleansed by a traitorous cup,
when you at last remember everything,
you see how Love and Art are yours,
how you were tricked into giving them away
to fools; the Love you awakened
sent to warm the glutton crowds;
Brunnhilde re-cast as Mrs to Mr Gibichung,
never to grace your own barren hearth.
Then at the surge, when wings of worth
flap with your just demand,
you are just as suddenly slain.
Your terminus erupts in raven wings
and the All-Father who could have saved you
does nothing. One funeral beat
will serve for all. Everything must fall.

2.
Now proud Brunnhilde,
the spiteful demi-goddess, comes,
armed with her timeless grace.
Whom have you killed? she asks
He brought the sun to your side,
you heard his songs, took me,
his freely given gift, in vain.
Come, light the pyre, indeed!
Burn all the souls in whom the hero died,
see if the withering youth in your breast
falls too, like his, when the world
envelops darkness for an age.
His loss has cost you me:
I'll be no muse for coward bards.
All art and song I strip from you.
Birds even shall be dumb.
Life without Siegfried
must teach you what you have lost.

There burns the maiden Art:
museums blaze, books fall
as leaves, a flaming trumpet
melts, and in the wake
no hearth on earth shall glow again.

The floods of time and folly
bear off the Ring, while gods
who thought themselves undying
turn to dust in an eye-blink.
Now humankind will worship
a wimp's god, a bloody thorn,
a bleating lamb, a sigil.

Go to the forest black, go where
no church steeple blights horizon.
Stand there, and on a breeze you hear
Brunnhilde's hymn
changelessly re-sung:
to have lived, or died,
in the love of the human best
is great, and answerless.

To Cyrnus

Adapted from the Greek of Theognis

My wings shall be the ones *you* use to fly
in passage over boundless sea and earth;
you'll hear your name adorning many lips —
a wished-for celebrant at banquet mirth
when youths in loveliness shall bid you sound
again your flute's melodious breath — *my* wings,
when you plunge darkling underground
into the melancholy house of death,
shall keep your honor bright, unperishing,
fit for undying fame in your name's breath.
You shall be the only one of your name
to rise above the seas and shores of Greece,
sweeping from isle to isle the rocky main,
needless of horse at last, effortlessly
drawn by Muses in their violet crowns.
Thus men to come, if they still sing (or earth
and sun abide!) shall know and cherish you
because I loved and kept these letters safe.
Yes, these are *my* wings you fly upon.

But what is left to me, when I give you to all?
Scorned by your beauty, I burn and fall!

What Men Are Like

All men are like that, you know,
defensive and brave for honor's sake,
proud of their whiskered privilege,
lord of domains so clearly marked
with the smell of themselves.
They bite the back of your neck
as if they really meant to stay,
arched like that, in the impossible pose
of thrust and domination.

It is not true,
though he fight hordes to assert it,
that you are his sole affinity.
Come night, the moon sees what he is,
lost mariner in search of isles,
driven by lunar gravity
to *them*, those aching Others lined
on the gap-toothed fences of night.
Sirens in alleyways, dark eyes
on the brows of garbage cans —
for him, adventure is everywhere.

All men, when such a lure
compels them to go, become
what all men ever are:
arch-back, puffy-tailed tomcats.

At First Sight

You are my Ring of Power,
The hurled strength of Thor's hammer,
The Chalice, Excalibur,
Swan-Knight, archangel bright,
Siegfried awash in the Magic Fire,
Tristan, The Green Man,
The Last Mohican at the wood's edge,
Golden-fleeced Jason, Perseus fleet
winged down with blade and polished shield.

And as for me, I am just a poet,
the sum of all the dreamers' words I read
and marked as my rude guides and talismen.
I was called Edmond Dantès once
before I became rich and vengeful.
I was Nemo at the helm of *The Nautilus*,
implacable enemy of unjust nations.
I was stern Morbius on far Altair
weighing the wisdom of the ancient Krell,
withholding love for the more-than-human.
Paul Verlaine was I once — three times
I regarded the young Rimbaud
through the clouded cafe window
and I walked away and returned
and I walked away and returned
before I dared introduce myself.
Forlorn I walked to a London's dawning,
betrayed by Bosie to my prison cell.
With mates I wept for slain Sarpedon,
beat my shield for Achaean Patroklus.
These hands for Emperor Hadrian carved
the first immortal marble Antinous.
I despaired of all love at the organ
I played beneath the Paris Opera.

I was the avatar of solitude.
Why does it shatter now in one hot breath,
one head-to-toe embrace reducing me
to volt, amp, and constituent atoms?

You are my Ring of Power,
The hurled strength of Thor's hammer,
The Chalice, Excalibur,
Swan-Knight, archangel bright.
Siegfried awash in Magic Fire,
Tristan, The Green Man,
The last Mohican at the wood's edge,
Golden-fleeced Jason, Perseus fleet
winged down with blade and polished shield.

WHEN THE VAMPIRE IS KING

There are immortal beings, but they are all evil.
Whereas we live on the substance of life, eating
the root and flesh of creatures, *they* live
on life itself, the force and essence of being.

One of their kind has come to me, and fed.
Before each dawn he will have come and gone again,
again and forever until my last breathing.
It is a slow death he brings; he is barely
existent, paper-thin. He will be at it for months,
pin-prick and red-dot scab so quickly gone,
I barely notice. He grows more solid each night.

My friends are little help. They are being finished off.
The vampire's minions have formed a gang: red-
hatted criminals in sports attire and fast cars.
Each victim is reduced to just a pile of bones,
so that I will be left alone for *his* stalking.
He turns the corner — I dash inside a doorway,
an empty apartment or untenanted warehouse.
The moment I reach its back-door egress, I find
him standing there, pale as an opossum.
He wags his finger in admonition: no exit
exists except I will find him already there.

On the dread night of the Winter Solstice I die,
and on the next morn he will assume a human form —
my youthful twin, solid and mirror-bright.
He will live out the life he stole from me.
His henchmen will be no encumbrance to his plan:
having devoured everyone I know, to the bone,
they will turn cannibal and consume each other.
Only my evil twin will be inheritor
of the desolate carnage of my existence.

On the dread night of the Winter Solstice I die,
unless there be other immortals who hate
that crispèd, crawling parasite enough
to rise from Tartarus to put him down.
Where is the hell-mouth, then? How to descend
into the darkness where evil hates itself
enough to foment a war of lesser monsters
against a great and ancient foe? Old books I seek,
the magic alchemical lore of my childhood,
a gateway talisman, the key that Solomon
and Dee and the other necromancers passed on.
The stone Eleggua winks at me as I incant:
Opener of Doorways, lead the way! Hecate,
scorn not the call of one who is not a woman!
Ye Hundred-Handed slayers, lend me but one hand!

I am not lamb, I am not sacrificial ox.
A vampire should be no more than a mosquito
to my larger and more expansive new self.
I shall return, then, from the onyx night of Hell
with bat-bane and wolf-bane and Gorgon shield,
and with the one sword that will open him
and free a thousand souls' life-force into the cosmos.

Vampire, stalk not a sorcerer!

ABOUT THE POEMS

THIS VOLUME CONTAINS all my poems and revisions from mid-2018 to Spring 2019, in the order they were written or revised. Amid the seeming randomness, readers may find some common threads. Some of the new poems come from dreams, or mental work done on dreams that occurred years ago, ripening until the words seemed ready to fall onto the page. In between the completely-new poems, I returned to poems that were published years ago, or left as thwarted sketches. In both new and old poems, the trouble of our times intrudes. American poets today, if not canaries in coal mines, share the sense of intellectual alarm that goes back millennia when states crumble, rights are trampled, and the mob raises its shaggy head, noose in hand.

THE GIRL ON THE LIBRARY STEPS comes from my native Scottdale, Pennsylvania, where the old library was on a second floor, and there was always a sense of ascending into a temple of books. I knew children whose parents hated books, and those sad memories are compressed into one little girl who seemed almost like a phantom haunting the stairwell.

THE DAY IS NORMAL IN MY CITY came to me the weekend when we first learned that migrants were being detained at the Mexican border, their children confined in cages. Cages. At the Pittsburgh Symphony that night, people in the symphony garden tried to act as though everything was normal. The poem's opening lines came to me in Spanish, the voice, as it were, of the people seeking asylum. After the poem was completed in Spanish, I did the English version. This is the first time I wrote a poem first in Spanish. A note of thanks to Vincent Spina for counsel on the Spanish.

WITH POE ON MORTON STREET PIER is from my *Anniversarius* autumn poem cycle. Two recent visits to Manhattan brought me back to the Hudson River in Greenwich Village, where there is no trace of the ruined piers and the somber atmosphere I knew in the 1970s. The revision clarifies the images but does not change the essential intent — walking in Poe's footsteps with as little money in my pocket as he had then.

LET THEM PLAY! is a tale from my Rutherford grandmother, told on the front-porch glider at an aunt's house. It is a legend known to the Onondaga Iroquois, a mother's advice about child-rearing inside a nightmarish horror story. In a time when powerful men abduct children in the name of the state, make what you will of my intent.

DEATH AND THE MAIDEN is the lyric by Matthias Claudius, used for Schubert's song, and from thence, for the powerful string quartet of the same name.

THE PLACE OF ATTICS compresses all the nastiness of New England, and Providence in particular, into one poem. As I told a Providence friend, "I could write a novel about New England attics, a novel about New England cellars, and a novella about the narrow passageways between buildings." This was based on an old sketch that I had suppressed – what it lacked was the full unleashing of anecdotes of Rhode Island awfulness. Some awfully fine people live there, still, but I wish them all a happier outcome.

Concerning AT THE EDGE OF THE LAKE, I posted the following on my blog: "I saw the lake, my lake, again, a few weeks ago [October 2018]. This brought me revisit this early poem, 'October 1967' from *The Pumpkined Heart*. We all thought the world was coming to an end soon. The Vietnam War divided the country. People were threatening 'hippies' with violence. In this 'nature poem,' written amid the violence of San Francisco's Haight-Ashbury, about the remembered lake and the carillon music from the bell tower, I felt the isolation and anxiety.
"Edinboro State College's carillon bells (real or a recorded) could be heard from afar. I remember going to class hearing 'Musetta's Waltz,' and coming out of class in the dark hearing Anton Rubinstein's haunting melody, 'Kammenoi Ostrow.' The memory of the Rubinstein music against a fall-winter horizon bleak enough to be Russian, stayed with me.
"Now I have rewritten this and added some current allusions, so that it is of 2018, although 95% of the poem is my 20-year-old voice speaking with the trees. This poem had been excluded from my *Anniversarius* autumn cycle, but this revision is now counted as part of that grouping."

GETTING YOUR EYE was from my early years in New York City, and was the kind of short lyric that our little Gothic-Romantic circle read to one another at Manhattan poetry readings, the kind of the poem that would leave someone shuddering and thinking, "Oh dear, was that about *me*?"

THE WITCHES AND THE HIGH-COURT JUDGE was my response to an Internet call for a hex on a certain obnoxious jurist. It is an adaptation of the "Song for Thirteen Witches" written by Ben Jonson in 1609 for his *Masque of Queens*. Those who followed the televised hearings will have learned about "bouffing," (beer funneled into one's backside), "running a train," (frat-boy gang sex assaults), the Devil's Triangle (two boys sharing one girl), and FFFF (look it up.)

THE CEMETERY AT EYLAU, 1807 is my adaptation of a war poem by Victor Hugo, "The Story of Louis-Joseph." I embellished a little on the explosions in the graveyard but is otherwise very close to Hugo's original. Although Hugo may have intended to portray bravery and loyalty, to the modern reader, it seems otherwise. Those who give the orders for battle ride off in triumph; those who take orders die foolish and horrifying deaths.

I revised THE TEA PARTY several times, and it makes a good companion piece to my poem, "Mrs. Friedman's Golem," in my collection, *Crackers At Midnight*. It's a sad thought that such people are still there, teaching their children the same hateful nonsense. I am glad I will not share hell with them.

FIRST H.P. LOVECRAFT WATERFIRE, PROVIDENCE is a blank-verse account of my visit to first Waterfire Festival honoring Providence's native son H.P. Lovecraft. The presentations were delightful, while the populace lived up to Howard's misanthropy and xenophobia. Perhaps I was channeling the Old Gent's detestation of crowds.

I DREAMT I WAS DANTE is from a very old sketch, based on a dream. A day after revising this poem, I chanced onto a photo of the supposed burial-place of Homer, and an anecdote about Homer being hounded to death by rowdy boys. So AT THE GRAVE OF HOMER spring into being in the same space as Dante. Its brevity evokes the classic Greek epigram.

THE DOLL WITHOUT A FACE came to me as a dream more than a decade ago, and I have related it several times to friends as an anecdote. Always the women's voices come to me, layered one behind another, with an intensity almost shattering. My grandmother, Olive Rutherford, known to us all as half-Indian, must have been told something by her mother, Mary White Trader, who had revealed in old age that she was a Native American raised by a German-American farm family. And that something might certainly have been how and when she lost touch with her own mother, as the local Mingo-Iroquois were driven west to Ohio. I have fleshed it out with the names of the Indian trails that the mother would have used to visit her daughter, and I made the faceless Iroquois doll the focal point of the narration. I will never know how much of this is "true." It is, nonetheless, true to the lived history of generations of people in my home-town of Scottdale.

During my New York City years, poet Barbara A. Holland and I founded and edited the city's first printed poetry calendar, titled *Poets Fortnightly*. This amusing poem, THE SORCERER'S COMPLAINT, was provoked by the fact that each Monday when Barbara arrived with copy, she was drenched from a rainfall. She liked this poem enough to write her own sequel to it, "Take Flight to Montreal."

THE WARNING was written immediately after awakening from a dream. Animals are now appearing all the time in my dreams, and they seem to be trying to tell me something.

A TOAST TO WENDY is an oral history of sorts, combining my memories with those of others who participated in the annual New Year's poetry gathering of the group now known as The Poets of the Palisades. It is a true account of a bizarre night at a New England bed-and-breakfast, and this poem memorializes all of our combined accounts which, only taken together, accumulate to the horrible revelation at the end.

THE POET WHO STARVED is adapted from the German of Ludwig Uhland (1787-1862). As the arts are de-funded, denigrated, and coarsened into noisy chaos, there must still be a poet who "raised his proud cup from afar."

BY THE ROMAN ROAD FORGOTTEN. In 1967, Russian poet Yevgenii Yevtushenko was part of an artistic delegation sent to Syria, and he was taken to see, outside Damascus, the remnants of an ancient Roman road. His guide did not know who built it or when. The Russian poet, writing in the time of Brezhnev, cast his poem as a subtle protest, using Rome and its decadence and cruelty as a stand-in for the Soviet rulers, ever-spreading their power over tributary states. I had started this translation twenty years ago, and then abandoned it. I felt compelled now to go back to it. We need protest poems against imperial ambitions more now than ever, and the thought that American troops were engaging with ISIS fighters on or near the same old Roman roads in Syria made it even more compelling. I have followed Yevtushenko's poem line-for-line, but I took the liberty of adding some lines about the actual history of the road, which was built in the time of the emperor Diocletian. The network of Roman roads, maintained in some places for more than 800 years, let the Roman armies dominate Europe and much of the Middle East. The poem resonates still, and holds out a beacon of warning.

AN OLD FLAME is my riff against Valentine's Day.

I have read a lot of German lyric poems on the last couple of years, and THE PARTISAN'S WOMAN is a poem in that vein. It has the manner of a ballad, without rhyming. I put into it my present political fears, as I have been telling people they'd better figure out whom they would hide, and who would hide them, if it came to that.

LOVE SONG IN FINLAND was translated from Goethe in the same mood. Goethe based his poem on a strange Finnish song, and I liked its dark images.

THROUGH MIRRORS is in the voice of a flaneur, watching the beautiful people in café mirrors.

ONLY AN APPLE is from the Greek poet Plato (not the philosopher).

I was honored to be Annette Hayn's publisher and friend for decades, and WHY POETRY? is based on her account to me of how and why she took up poetry in mid-life. It also recaps her childhood in Nazi Germany and her family's escape to England and America.

THE WARNING OF SOLON THE ATHENIAN is adapted from the Greek. This speech, attributed to the great Solon, is taken from a speech of Demosthenes, where he recites Solon's words from memory.

The preceding poem, and THE RAGE OF ATHENA AT TROY, were part of a pageant-play, *Who Is Athena?* I wrote for The Providence Athenaeum in 2008, to install a bust of Athena. Not many poets get invited to write pageant-plays, so it was an honor to troll through Greek literature for anecdotes about or invoking Athena. This fragment from Euripides is book-ended by the pageant's narrator and the pageant's Greek chorus. As a poem, it presents the capricious wrath of the gods.

WRITER'S BLOCK was written many years ago, and it is in the vein of those poems that Barbara A. Holland and I wrote in dialogue using the imagery of the paintings of Rene Magritte. Magritte's mysterious stone slabs dropped onto a cityscape were the direct stimulus for one of these inscrutable stones being a "writer's block." I held this poem back until now, and the current version is, I think, sufficiently clear to separate itself from the Magritte world. It's also a memory of life in the West Village.

OUT-HOME SUMMERS started as a little clump of poems in dialogue with my friend Claudia Dikinis, sometimes around 1975. They were not much more than brief images recalled from childhood. The locale is my grandmother's tiny house on Ore Mine Hill Road outside Scottdale, Pennsylvania. The fourth poem moves to nearby Hecla, a coal-patch town where we lived at the coke ovens during the summer of Hurricane Hazel.

WHO CARES TO LISTEN TO SONGS? is a translation from Anna Akhmatova. The last two lines seem of the present, do they not?

A HAIGHT-ASHBURY AUTUMN, a revision, may be the oldest poem in this volume. It appeared in my early book, *Songs of the I and Thou*, and recalls my 1967 sojourn in San Francisco.

THE PLASMA PHYSICIST EXPLAINS is yet another love poem couched in scientific terminology. It is a lonely, shy confession.

ON RHYMING POETRY. I seldom employ rhyme. I have published a few books of formal poems by others, when I was satisfied that they employed rhyme as only one of many poetic devices, and that they could write fluidly in rhyme. Listening to doggerel verse, hard end-rhyming poems, and anything in that vein, is literally painful for me. My aversion was shared by most of my Greenwich Village poet friends, and I remember reading this parody of Barbara A. Holland's famous "Black Sabbat" poem. People who knew her work groaned and laughed. I added a few new lines at the end to make the point.

WOTAN AND SIEGFRIED is one of two Wagner-inspired poems in this book. The arrogant youth encounters the one-eyed All-Father, and all does not go well. The ironic exchange between god and hero was too wonderful to pass up.

AT THE TOP OF THE WORLD has been revised several times over the years. It is a bit Nietzschean, I suppose, a call for heroes to shun the world and to look down in scorn on war and brutality. "Thin air and star-glory, cloud-food and fog/ are now your homeland." I think I have finally made in into the exile's anthem I wanted it to be.

THE AUTUMN FUNGUS was written after seeing shelf fungus devouring the trunk of one of Providence's beautiful copper beech trees. One by one, people have allowed these giants to rot and fall. To the delight of real estate developers.

CONGRESS, IN RECESS could be any Congress, any year.

THE VIRGIN MARY, AFTER ONE VIEW OF THE KAMA SUTRA is a revision of a long-suppressed poem. The original was simply an ekphrastic lyric about the Campin painting at The Cloisters in New York, in which I expressed some skepticism about the Virgin's willingness, and some horror at the image of the tiny Jesus and cross flying toward her womb like a battering ram. By elaborating on this idea with some humor, and focusing on a "Flemish Maria" contemporaneous with the painting, I was able finally, to make this a finished poem. Doubtless, the Grand Inquisitor will be looking into this.

THE RETURN OF RICHARD NIXON was written years ago, and just needed a little updating. And for some reason we are talking more and more about the slithery return of shamed politicians. What used to be called a "decent interval" is now like a dog turning three times in the high grass.

MOVING DAY was written after returning to Providence from Weehawken, and then revised again as I reflected on my last departure from Providence for Pittsburgh. I have moved a horrifying number of times over the years. Get this: Edinboro – San Francisco – Edinboro – New York – Newark – New York – Edinboro — New York — Brooklyn – New York – Weehawken – Providence – Weehawken – Providence – Boston – Brooklyn –Weehawken – Providence – Pittsburgh.

LIFE WITHOUT SIEGFRIED is a kind of hallucinogenic take on attending a Carnegie Hall concert, with the Chicago Symphony under Sir Georg Solti, performing the last act of *Götterdämmerung*. The absence of staging and costumes let the mind roam free.

My earliest adaptation of a poem from Greek is this poignant love poem by Theognis, TO CYRNUS. It pretty much set the tone for my doomed romantic life.

WHAT MEN ARE LIKE is a cynical counterpoise to the Greek poem.

In AT FIRST SIGHT, the old poet finds himself unaccountably smitten. A moment of weakness, briefly encouraged, and then, as the Flying Dutchman averred, "Back to sea, forever!"

WHEN THE VAMPIRE IS KING, the newest and latest poem in this volume, fell onto the page in the moments after I awoke from a dream. It is what I was able to scribble down, only a small outline of an elaborate story. It has a Shelleyan edge of defiance to it, and makes it a suitable curtain for this collection of follies.

About the Poet

BRETT RUTHERFORD, BORN in Scottdale, Pennsylvania, began writing poetry seriously during a stay in San Francisco. During his college years at Edinboro State College in Pennsylvania, he published an underground newspaper and printed his first hand-made poetry chapbook. He moved to New York City, where he founded The Poet's Press in 1971. For more than twenty years, he worked as an editor, journalist, printer, and consultant to publishers and nonprofit organizations.

After a literary pilgrimage to Providence, Rhode Island, on the track of H.P. Lovecraft and Edgar Allan Poe, he moved there with his press. *Poems From Providence* was the fruit of his first three years in the city (1985-1988), published in 1991. Since then, he has written a study of Edgar Allan Poe and Providence poet Sarah Helen Whitman (briefly Poe's fiancée), a biographical play about Lovecraft, and his second novel, *The Lost Children* (Zebra Books, 1988). His poetry, in volumes both thematic and chronological, can be found in *Poems From Providence* (1991, 2011), *Things Seen in Graveyards* (2007, 2017), *Twilight of the Dictators* (1992, 2009), *The Gods As They Are, On their Planets* (2005, 2012, 2018), *Prometheus on Fifth Avenue* (1987, 2018), *Whippoorwill Road: The Supernatural Poems* (1995, 1998, 2005, 2008, 2012), *An Expectation of Presences* (2012), *Trilobite Love Song* (2014), and *Crackers At Midnight* (2017).

Returning to school for a master's degree in English, Rutherford completed this project in 2007, and worked for University of Rhode Island in distance learning, and taught for the Gender and Women's Studies Department. There, he created courses on "The Diva," "Women in Science Fiction," and "Radical American Women."

He has prepared annotated editions of Matthew Gregory Lewis's *Tales of Wonder*, the poetry of Charles Hamilton Sorley, A.T. Fitzroy's antiwar novel *Despised and Rejected*, the four-volume collected writings of Emilie Glen, and the literary essays and selected poems of Sarah Helen Whitman. A number of his book chapters and critical essays and articles can be found on academia.edu. New poems-in-progress and other writings can be found at brettrutherford.blogspot.com.

His interests include classical music and opera, and Latin American music; classics and mythology; Chinese art, history and literature; bicycling, graveyards, woods, horror films, intellectual history, and crimes against nature.

Retiring from his workaday life in early 2016, Rutherford moved to the Squirrel Hill neighborhood in Pittsburgh, where he continues to write, to study music, to run The Poet's Press, and to evade capture by the thought police.

ABOUT THIS BOOK

The body text for this book is set in Plantin. Several attractive modern fonts, including Galliard and Plantin, are based on typefaces originally designed by Robert Granjon (1513-1589), a prolific type designer and founder active in Paris, in the shop of Christopher Plantin, and later in Rome at the Vatican. In 1913, Monotype issued several versions, some based on Granjon's designs.

Poem titles are set in Goudy Catalogue. This heavier version of Frederic Goudy's Old Style typeface was designed by Morris Fuller Benton for American Typefounders in 1919, adding the italic version in 1921. Main titles and section titles are in Goudy Stout.

The cover art features a NASA photo of the Pleiades and a digital-art rendering of an Iroquois doll. The book is ornamented with digital art renderings of dried woven corn husks. The digital-art doll was inspired by an Onondaga doll crafted by the late clan mother Dorothy Hill Webster.

The Annuniciation, on display at The Metropolitan Museum of Art, The Cloisters, in New York City, is part of the Merode Altarpiece (1425-1428), an oak panel triptych. The work is attributed to Dutch painter Robert Campin and assistants. Image from Wikimedia Commons.

www.ingramcontent.com/pod-product-compliance
Lightning Source LLC
Chambersburg PA
CBHW051654040426
42446CB00009B/1131